BLACKPOOL'S
HAUNTED
HERITAGE

BLACKPOOL'S HAUNTED HERITAGE

Ghostly Tales from Britain's Scariest Seaside Town

By JASON KARL
& ADELE YEOMANS

First published in 2009
by Palatine Books,
Carnegie House,
Chatsworth Road
Lancaster LA1 4SL
www.palatinebooks.com

Researcher Willow Silverwheel

British Library Cataloguing-in-Publication data
A catalogue record for this book is available from the British Library

ISBN 10: 1-874181-65-9
ISBN 13: 978-1-874181-65-1

Designed and typeset by Carnegie Book Production
www.carnegiebookproduction.com

Printed and bound in the UK by Short Run Press, Exeter

CONTENTS

INTRODUCTION

Welcome to Britain's spookiest seaside resort – Blackpool, renowned for its sweet candy rock, landmark tower, friendly guesthouses and live entertainment. But peer behind the phantom façade of bright lights and fast food and you will find a different side to Blackpool; a world where the ghosts of yesteryear lurk in the shadows. Ghosts in theatres, hotels, pubs, houses and halls, where the boundary between the realm of the living and the dead is thin, and for those who dare, a brush with Blackpool's spectres is but a few steps away.

As the hoards of beach-bronzed bodies parade the promenade by day, and fill the nightspots by night, spare a thought for those who have gone before, now nothing more than a subtle vibration in Black-pool's etheric otherworldly aura, which can be sensed, and sometimes seen, by those who seek them out ...

In this, the second book in the *Haunted Heritage* series, we delved deep into paranormal happenings recorded in and around Blackpool, from the friendly phantom of the Grand Theatre, and the strange tales of Windmill Cottage, to the dancing ghosts of the Empress Ballroom and 'Cloggy' who haunts the world famous Ghost Train at Blackpool Pleasure Beach, we have searched high and low for tales of twisted terrors in the town of seaside spirits.

This frightfully fun guide includes both hilarious and horrific ghostly tales of all kinds, written in a colourful style that is intended to inform and entertain the reader. *Blackpool's Haunted Heritage* is also a permanent record, chronicling for posterity these fantastic tales which might otherwise be forgotten in years to come. The reader is reminded that this is neither an academic nor a comprehensive study; it is instead a lighthearted jaunt through the tales, many of which may be considered 'tall', that can be found in Blackpool and its surrounding districts. Although some of the stories are already well known in local legend, we have included many brand new ones to delight the avid spectre hunter, along with a fresh look at some of the established haunts.

As summer draws to a close each year and the tourist season inevitably comes to an end, it is then, in the autumn and winter months, that the quiet waves brush over the pebbles where so many have walked, and the spirits come out of their old haunts, revisiting happy times in Blackpool. The shades of glory days are still bound to their earthly haunting grounds in this sometimes spookily quiet ghost town.

Next year we will begin investigating the city of Lancaster for the third book in the *Haunted Heritage* series, and we would be delighted to hear of any ghostly tales we might include … But in the meantime dim the lights, close the curtains and sit back as we explore the shadowy side of Britain's scariest seaside town, in *Blackpool's Haunted Heritage*.

Happy hauntings!

Jason Dexter Karl
www.jasondexterkarl.com

ACKNOWLEDGEMENTS

We would like to thank;
All at Carnegie Publishing and Palatine Books for believing in the
Haunted Heritage project, and for allowing us to pursue our ghostly
pursuits around Blackpool and its surrounding districts.
The researcher on this project, Willow Silverwheel of AtmosFEAR!
    Scare Attractions
The owners, curators, innkeepers and custodians of the locations
    featured in the book
Julia Bennett at the *Blackpool Gazette*
Stephen Mercer at the Grand Theatre, Blackpool
Roger Yeomans at Mains Hall, Poulton-le-Fylde
Debi Clark for her account of the ghost at 'Jumper'
Laura Eastham and Kevin Cook at Blackpool Pleasure Beach
Wilky Dee for his accounts of the Grundy Art Gallery and the Royal
    Pavilion Theatre
James Young for the story of the Carleton ghost
Christina Bedford for her tale of Layton Hill Convent
Sheila and Brian Smithall of Windmill Cottage
Roger Griffiths and Frances Green for Lily's Story
David Summerville (good luck with your new book) for his account
    of the Mains Hall dovecote
Edith Finlayson for her account of the Lobster Pot haunting
Jonathan and Debbie Kozakiewicz, Abigail and Darren Woodcock,
    Suzanne Stuttle, Lily Isherwood and Barbara Woolford for their
    tales of The Grapevine
Paul Hurst at The Shard Riverside Inn

CHAPTER ONE

FRIGHT-FILLED FUN

THE PLEASURE BEACH, BLACKPOOL

As you may expect, the Ghost Train at Blackpool is home to a variety of plastic spooks set to jump out as the cars whizz through its dimly lit tunnels, but it is also home to a ghost of a different kind – that of a former ride operator, now one of Blackpool's most famous ghosts, nicknamed 'Cloggy'.

One of the park's favourite rides, it was created in 1930 by a Japanese entrepreneur named Mr Kamiya and originally named the 'Pretzel Ride'. When the Pleasure Beach acquired it, they renamed it the 'Ghost Train', after Joseph Emberton rebuilt it ready for debut in Blackpool in 1936. The name derived from a popular stage production of the same name which was taking the West End by storm at the time, and the universal 'ghost train' term, now applied to similar rides all over the world, was born.

Ride workers who have to walk the track late at night performing maintenance checks and repairs, have reported feeling as if they are not alone, and the sound of footsteps has been heard echoing around the dark tunnels when there are no staff members in the ride. Danny Moore, an electrical supervisor at the attraction, says he has witnessed several odd things while working on the Ghost Train, one being the illumination of the lights inside a large prop skull which perches atop the ride building. When he went to see why they had been turned on he was surprised to find the power had already been turned off, in theory rendering them inoperable!

The activity is thought to be caused by the ghost of a friendly ride operator who used to work the Ghost Train in the 1970s, whom colleagues remember always wore a pair of clogs, giving rise to the nick-name.

We spent a night inside the Ghost Train ride in 2002 with psychic medium Derek Acorah and a camera crew, and although the spectre of Cloggy failed to put in an appearance on that particular evening it is easy to understand why staff members may get 'spooked' when alone inside the spooky attraction at night. The atmosphere pierced our objective veneer on more than one occasion as a styrofoam skull or bat flew into our unsuspecting faces!

The Pleasure Beach itself has a colourful past and dates back to 1896. It is built over a site formerly inhabited by Romany gypsies and with over 100 years of history, it is not surprising to hear that there are several other seaside spectres haunting the park. By day the Pleasure Beach is filled with the sounds of laughter and the scent of candy floss, but by night a far more sinister aura envelops the older parts of Blackpool's premier tourist venue.

Kevin Cook, a security guard at the Pleasure Beach reported: 'I regularly patrol the park alone at night when the visitors have left, accompanied by a guard dog. On many occasions I have been unable to persuade the dog to enter the Paradise Room in the art deco White Tower building; he just stops on the threshold and starts barking as if he is being challenged. I have been told that a ghost known as 'Albert' haunts the area'.

We contacted Laura Eastham at the Pleasure Beach in 2001 and she told us of several other haunted hotspots around the complex. Sir Hiram Maxim's Gift Shop sits underneath the Flying Machine ride, which is the oldest attraction in the park. The shop has been open since the ride opened in 1904 and is reputedly haunted by the spirit of a 9-year-old girl. Shop merchandise moves around overnight and has been known to be thrown with force across the shop, or even levitate off the shelves. In 1998 a particular new product was obviously disliked by the ghost; it continually moved to a different spot in the building each night until staff stopped forcing the issue and gave in to the ghost – leaving the item permanently where she had moved it too! When the spirit has been seen it has always

manifested in the farthest end of the shop from the front doors. While spending some time at night inside the shop some objects were set up in the hope that they might have moved inexplicably, but as is often the case, the spectral child refused to play and left them exactly where they had been placed.

The Star pub has been on the site since the 1930s and is haunted by a bearded figure described by the two workmen who saw it in 1996 as looking like Karl Marx, having a large beard and being dressed in clothing reminiscent of the 1890s. The workmen were busy with renovation of the bar which had recently been acquired by the

Pleasure Beach when they saw the strange man, but when they looked back moments later he had vanished into thin air. The same ghost was seen again a year later at 3 a.m. walking through one of the bars and then disappearing. The identity of this phantom figure remains unknown, and staff still continue to refuse to enter the cellar alone to this day, reporting that a foggy cloud appears there, accompanied by a feeling of deep unease.

The Ice Drome, now known as the Arena, also has its fair share of ghostly tales, the primary spook being that of a male spectre referred to as 'Julian' by some sources. Anecdotal accounts report a feeling of 'bone chilling sensations' and 'presence' felt in the building, where thousands watch spectacular ice shows every day during the season. Of course one might expect 'coldness' to permeate the bones here, after all it is filled with ice, but that cannot explain the visual and sound phenomena which have also been reported. These range from a man manifesting in the centre of the ice stage and walking out of the side exit, to the sound of a spectral skater who leaves grooves in the freshly frozen ice, the latter being reported by more than one person. One former Ice Drome worker tells of dressing-room doors being unlocked overnight, and another, who worked as a skater during the 1970s, tells of a fatal accident when a performer fell to his death from the high wire during a live show – perhaps it is his restless ghost that remains here?

Louis Tussaud's Waxworks, Blackpool

Louis Tussaud, grandson of the great Madame Tussaud, first came to the seaside resort of Blackpool at the turn of the twentieth century. He had decided to tour the country setting up his waxworks show for all to enjoy after a devastating fire had left him bereft of his London premises. He chose the basement of the Hippodrome theatre on Church Street as the host venue for his slightly macabre lifelike figurines, but he was not the first waxworks showman in Blackpool; that title belongs jointly to Monsieur D'Arc and Elias Fletcher, whose exhibits were housed near Central Pier in the 1870s, and later in 1890 Mr Lee's 'Grand Museum and Royal Waxwork' was opened near the

Grand Theatre, Louis took advantage of the precedent set by these earlier entertainers in wax and opened his own showcase in July 1900. A year later he moved his collection to the Golden Mile.

The Tussaud collection was later acquired by former Blackpool mayor Albert Lindsay Parkinson, and he combined the exhibition with a second waxworks exhibit giving the new attraction the famous 'Tussaud' label, and housing it in a building on Wellington Terrace until 1928. In 1929 Lindsay Parkinson's building firm constructed the building on the Golden Mile where it remains open to visitors today. From its early heyday stretching back over the last century, a 'chamber of horrors' exhibit has always been a popular part of the exhibition, but it is not just the lifeless manikins that send a shivery chill up the spine today; for the building is home to a ghost named 'Carol', and the site of a very strange photograph which seems to defy rational explanation.

The photograph in question was sent to the internationally acclaimed researcher Dale Kaczmarek of the Ghost Research Society in the USA and it can be viewed on their website. It was taken by Pauline Brannigan in August 2005 and appears to show a ghoulish blue face staring out of a window in the *Coronation Street* section of the museum. According to the statement written by Pauline and published on the Ghost Research Society website, nothing was seen at the time of the exposure which can explain the face, and so she sent it to the management of the attraction for further explanation. Unable to explain the peculiar image, the photograph has since gone down in the history of ghost photography as a possible example of a spirit extra.

Examining the picture, it is clearly similar in appearance to an actress named Violet Carson, who portrayed the fictional character of Ena Sharples for twenty years in the soap, from its beginning in 1960. A tentative connection can be made with Blackpool as she was a native of the town. She died peacefully in her sleep in 1983 following an illness.

There has been much speculation as to the authenticity of the image, which some say could be a photographic still from the programme, or a television screen housed behind the glass front of the Rover's Return set where the ghostly face appears to be looking out from. Either way it is an interesting tale from an attraction with an interesting past, and well worth a visit – if you spot Ena (or Carol) be sure to let us know!

THE TOWER, BLACKPOOL

Arguably Blackpool's most famous landmark, the Tower was originally opened on 14th May 1894. It stands proudly at the centre of the resort and rises 158 metres into the sky, making it visible from 30 miles away in Lancaster, Liverpool, Preston and Southport, and it acts as a central landmark and focal point for the entire town.

The Tower was commissioned by Mayor John Bickerstaffe after he had viewed the Eiffel Tower during the Great Paris Exhibition of 1889, which inspired him to set up a consortium of businessmen and invest £2000 of his own money to form the Blackpool Tower Company Ltd. Work on the design began and James Maxwell and Charles Tuke, two

architects from Lancashire, were assigned the task of bringing the company's vision to life and the building's foundation stone was laid on September 29th 1891. Sadly, by the time the Tower finally opened to the public in 1894, both men had died.

It is in the Tower Ballroom that much of the haunting activity occurs. The original ballroom was known as the Tower Pavilion and opened in August 1894, but it was judged too small, and in response to the opening of the elaborate Empress Ballroom at the Winter Gardens, a larger, grander version was designed for the Tower. The architect was Frank Matcham, who also designed the Grand Theatre. His new masterpiece ballroom opened in 1899, an enchanting room of carved mahogany, oak and walnut and lit by stunning crystal chandeliers. The room has a worldwide reputation and has been used to stage many television and theatrical production including the BBC's *Come Dancing*.

The first Wurlitzer organ was installed in 1929, and its sound has become synonymous with Blackpool entertainment, but it is not just during the hours of daylight, when tea dances and shows draw crowds to the ballroom, that you might hear its haunting melody ... Late at night, the distinct sound of the organ can sometimes be heard when the tourists and dancers have long gone. Many walk away, afraid of what they might encounter if they enter the grand chamber, but those who have dared to brave the shadows if the hall have reported watching the silent shades of spectral ballroom dancers whirling around the floor; a momentary spectral glimpse of a forgotten yesteryear. Here also, footsteps fall in a deserted balcony where no human walks, and the shadows cast by the huge chandeliers sometimes move of their own accord, as if the unseen are flitting gleefully among their sentient counterparts. Tales also are told of chairs moving mysteriously overnight, when no staff members have been present.

It seems to us that passion, joy and happiness sometimes leave an imprint in the fabric of places we have loved and rejoiced in, just as intense sadness, anger and hate can leave their own phantom imprint. In a room where so many have sung, danced and laughed it is not surprising that the shades of those from the past return to this happy haunting ground from time to time, to savour once again the delights of the Tower Ballroom.

BLACKPOOL ZOO, BLACKPOOL

Perhaps the most unlikely of all haunted hotspots in the town, Blackpool Zoo has a heritage of paranormal incidences stretching back several years. But it's not the ghosts of former zoo animals which perambulate around the site in the dark hours, but the phantoms of long dead airmen from the first half of the twentieth century.

Back in 1931 the zoo site was the home of the original Blackpool Municipal Aerodrome, a busy location with an interesting history. At the outset of the Second World War the RAF requisitioned the aerodrome and thousands of airmen were trained there. Additional buildings were constructed to assemble Wellington bombers, but at the end of the war the site was closed; no-one ever flew from there again.

The zoo opened to the public in 1972 and was built over the aerodrome site, incorporating many of the existing old buildings into its infrastructure: the air traffic control tower was rebuilt as zoo offices and the hangars became animal pens and storage areas.

The haunting activity centres around the old hangars and aerodrome buildings, with the keepers' flats and Elephant House having the most incidences of supernatural activity.

According to reports given to the *Blackpool Gazette*, late at night the sound of stamping feet can sometimes be heard in the old hangars, and zoo staff have also watched lights inexplicably switch on of their own accord, heard music in deserted rooms and felt as if they are not alone, being observed by unseen eyes …

Medium Christine Hawkes was asked to investigate the haunting activity to try to understand exactly who was responsible for the phenomena; following her investigation she concluded that the site was filled with eerie energies from the past, and that these were causing the sounds and sights described as ghosts by the staff.

THE ILLUMINATIONS DEPOT, BLACKPOOL

Famous throughout the world as the most dazzling light show in Britain, the Blackpool Illuminations entertain and delight thousands of visitors every autumn. As the leaves turn brown and fall to the ground, so the spectacle of light and colour brings Blackpool back to life. But there is a darker side to the bright lights of the tableaux, and it seems that the maintenance depot on Rigby Road houses more than bulbs and cables ...

Psychic investigations have been conducted at the site since 2005 when Derek Acorah visited with a film crew, and since then local investigators have taken up the challenge. All have found evidence that the workshops and storage facilities might be haunted.

A feeling of sudden cold and the sensation of being watched while working late at night have been reported by several staff members. In April 2008 Peter Parr, who is a manager at the depot, told local reporter Julia Bennett that he had heard the footsteps of a former employee who had passed on while working in the sheds.

Another suggestion posed by the ghost hunters is that the spectre is the victim of a donkey accident in 1915 – the depot is housed on the former site of sheds for the donkeys which used to entertain people along the seafront decades ago.

CHAPTER TWO

STUDIOUS SPECTRES

The Grundy Art Gallery, Blackpool

The Grundy Art Gallery on Queen Street, a beautiful example of Edwardian architecture, was commissioned by Blackpool Council in 1908 as a home for artworks of merit. It opened to the public in 1911 and now houses temporary and permanent exhibitions for all to enjoy. It is, or was, haunted by the ghost of Preston portrait artist Patti Mayor.

Wilky Dee, star of stage and screen, provided the following account of a remarkable experience he shared with members of the ghost's family in the mid nineties, when he was incumbent as the Gallery's fine painting restorer.

Wilky had always been a showman, for years travelling the world as a stage hypnotist with his assistant Danielle, playing summer seasons in far off places in the sun, and residencies in some of Blackpool's busiest theatres. But in the mid 1990s he decided it was time for a change. Wilky had always harboured a love of art and as an accomplished painter himself he was able to turn his hand to restoring great masterpieces that had succumbed to the ravages of time. It was this rare skill that lead him to the Grundy Art Gallery where the council were seeking to employ a new restorer.

On his first day Wilky was given a huge bunch of keys and set about exploring the various galleries and store rooms scattered throughout the vast structure. It was in one of these darkened holding rooms that he came across a collection of old paintings, dusted with cobwebs and bowing with age, their fine, gilded plasterwork frames smashed into smithereens upon the floor. There was one painting in particular which caught his eye, a small head and shoulders portrait of a young lady, badly damaged and with a gaping hole next to the subjects ear. There was something enchanting about the picture which mesmerized him and he made it his mission to restore the painting without delay.

Upon closer inspection he discovered that the painting bore the signature of Patti Mayor, a little-known portrait artist from Preston, who had bequeathed a collection of 45 paintings to the gallery upon her death, in thanks for the exhibition they had granted her there during her lifetime. Wilky selected a further fifteen of Patti's portraits, all in need of restoration, and decided that he would give them the attention they rightly deserved in a new exhibition.

After the repairs where completed, the gallery opened a new exhibition. In order to create some PR spin, and attract visitors, he compiled a press release which he sent, along with some photographic examples, to the local newspapers in the north west, asking if they would ask their readers if they knew who the subjects of any of the paintings were. It was an instant success; telephone calls, visitors and letters flooded in, all telling Wilky about the artist and her intriguing past ...

According to the anecdotes and tales he was told by a variety of people who had known her, Patti lived in Preston for much of her life, with her sister. She painted young ladies from the mills as a hobby and as an activity to occupy her time. She never charged her sitters, but always kept the paintings for herself. By now, Wilky had become absorbed by Patti's life, and began recording the various stories people had told him for posterity.

Two of the most interesting visitors to the gallery were a couple from Cleethorpes who told Wilky that they had been related to Patti, and at one time had lived with her in a Victorian house in Preston. Wilky wasted no time in telling them what a rare gift she had for working with oils in such a brilliant fashion, and they seemed rather surprised, telling him that they had never really understood that she had much of a skill during her lifetime. They brought with them a photograph of a small exhibition she had given in Preston,

and another of the lady herself, which they gave to Wilky to keep, and told him that they had a large amount of her paintings stored in their loft in Cleethorpes. Wilky seized the opportunity to ask if they might be willing to allow him to borrow some of them, for inclusion in the gallery exhibition, but he was informed that they were in a bad state of decay and would not be suitable. Wilky explained that he was a restorer and agreed that if they allowed him to borrow the artworks he would restore them to their former glory and arrange to have them professionally framed. They were delighted with his offer and invited him to their home to view Patti's paintings as soon as possible.

The following Monday, Wilky made the trip from Blackpool to Cleethorpes. When he arrived he was presented with a barrage of works to choose from, as each chair, table and shelf displayed the dishevelled works of the couple's Aunt Patti. All were in a terrible state of disrepair and many had been rolled up, causing the paint to split and flake off. It was obvious that he could not undertake the mammoth task of restoring them all, so he selected eight which he felt best showcased Patti's talent, including one partially completed work which gave valuable clues as to her method of painting.

When Wilky returned to Blackpool it was too late to take the paintings to the gallery and so he took them home for the evening; it was then that a strange set of circumstances began to unfold.

That night, while trying to sleep, Wilky was haunted by visions of Patti's artworks and glimpses of the life he had been told she lead. An eerie feeling, which made his hair stand on end, invaded his otherwise peaceful flat, like some shadowy presence.

The following morning he left for the gallery to begin what should have been a month-long task of restoring his latest acquisitions. But as soon as he began his hands seemed to be possessed, working at great speed and instinctively knowing what to do.

By Saturday afternoon his task was complete. The seven new paintings, and one incomplete work, were fully restored, an achievement he is unable to explain even to this day. How had he managed the huge task of repairing so many paintings in so little time? Was it, as Wilky believes, the spectral hand of Patti Mayor, assisting his brushstrokes from beyond the grave?

A few days later, the framing was complete, and each image was displayed in a suitably exquisite frame with protective glass. In no time at all the paintings were hung in the exhibition for all to see, and Wilky telephoned his generous patrons from Cleethorpes to invite them to view his work. Astounded and pleased by the news that he had completed the restoration already, they agreed to come at once.

They were suitably impressed with the additions to the exhibition, and delighted to see their late aunt's work being so beautifully displayed. As they were admiring the finer points of the paintings, a family group came into the gallery. Wilky, with his usual courtesy and enthusiasm, went to greet them and enquired if they had known anything of Patti Mayor. "Why yes", they exclaimed, telling him that they had been related to the lady herself. "So are those people over there!" replied Wilky, indicating the couple from Cleethorpes over the other side of the room, and proceeded to introduce them to each other. Strangely, despite being members of the same family, they had never met.

After enquiring why the two families did not know each other, a tragic tale of love and deceit emerged ... It began in Victorian France, where, as a young artist, Patti travelled each summer to Paris. Here she painted portraits of tourists, while her sister played the piano and sang merry tunes in the bars and cafés. She met, and fell hopelessly in love with, a dashing young French painter, but their romance was doomed from the beginning. With little money to support themselves Patti was reliant on her father back in Preston, but he was unhappy about their relationship and after travelling to Paris to confront her, he delivered an ultimatum that if she did not return to England with him immediately she would be cut out of his will and thus inherit nothing of the family's vast fortune. Patti's father owned a large business empire manufacturing tarpaulins in Preston, and his attitude toward the foreigner was very Victorian. With little choice she reluctantly followed his wishes and never saw the Frenchman again; her true love, lost forever more.

It was a high price to pay, for years later, after her father had passed away, the business was passed not to his son, as was expected, but to a nephew, causing outrage within the family and leaving Patti and her sister with little money.

But this is not just a sad tale of lost love and a fragmented family; it is a tale of a great artist never recognised as such during her lifetime, but whose spirit lives on in her great paintings. Wilky believes that it was her ghost that drew him to the portrait in the storeroom, and which engineered the succession of strange events which ultimately lead to the reunion of her family, a spiritual quest to right an old wrong before finally resting in peace.

THE LIBRARY, LYTHAM

Lytham library on Clifton Street is an interesting Victorian building. It began its life in 1878 as a Mechanics Institute, offering a mixture of educational classes, apparatus for training purposes and a small library of books. In those early days it was maintained solely by public subscription.

The building was extended in 1898 to celebrate Queen Victoria's Diamond Jubilee, with a new reading room, gymnasium and further classrooms. In the early 1900s the library became part of the Municipal Borough of Lytham St Annes and in 1974 the administration of the library was taken over by Lancashire County Council.

An unusual tale has emerged since library staff there have been endeavouring to investigate who or what might be at the centre of their unique haunting. As well as the ubiquitous heavy footsteps heard in parts of the building where no-one is working and members of the public do not have access to, there is an odd poltergeist activity taking place, with objects being hurled around in the library. It appears that in one particular area of the library, 'Albert', as he has become affectionately known, ejects DVDs from their shelves. Barrie Mallinson, a cleaner at the library, seemed to be at the centre of some of Albert's fury, as he frequently fires them in his direction.

Other staff members had to put up with their computers going crazy and lights going off and on whilst they were trying to work. Odd smells were also reported during these times of intense poltergeist activity – ranging from the smell of burnt candles to fresh candy floss!

Librarian Elaine Bevan was so alarmed at some of the activity that

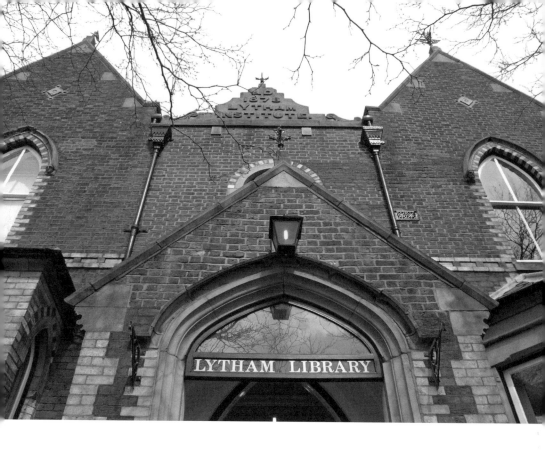

she called in a spiritualist medium to get to the bottom of who this phantom of the library might be, and more importantly, what was upsetting him so. Christine Hawkins from South Shore, Blackpool, tuned in to the spirit of a large stocky man wearing Victorian clothing. He was leaning against the fireplace in the library and shouting at all and sundry to, 'Go away, this is my home!' clearly under the impression that this was still his home and these were strangers who were in it. He also talked about wanting an apology from those who had, it seemed, taken his home away from him.

It was not until the librarians working there did some further research that they discovered that in fact there had been a row of cottages in the street behind the 'new' Victorian Mechanics Institute which we know was later extended in 1898. Some of these cottages were obviously demolished in this endeavour, much to Albert's obvious distaste. Staff there now leave Albert the occasional bunch of flowers on the mantelpiece – it is their way of saying sorry to him. Let's hope he's happy with this apology, if not you might need to be careful next time you go to choose a DVD from Lytham Library!

ST MARY'S CATHOLIC COLLEGE, BLACKPOOL

St Mary's Catholic College is a school with an interesting past. Founded in its current position in 1870, the sisters of the Society of the Holy Child Jesus had previously set up a school in Raikes Hall, Raikes Parade (now The Raikes Hotel public house] and it had been flourishing there since 1860. By 1870, however, the school had grown so much that they relocated to what was then known as Layton Hill, at that time, a desolate plot of land on St Walburgas Road, Layton. The school was re-founded and given the new name of Layton Hill Convent. It was initially a boarding school for Catholic girls, but in 1880 the nuns were encouraged to take in boys too. However, only two years later, the boys were moved to another location in Park Road, and this school became known as St Joseph's College for boys. Eventually, as the modern world dictated, Layton Hill Convent merged once again with St Joseph's around 1924, at a time when the Diocese of Lancaster (which Blackpool became a part of) required that all Catholic schools become co-educational. Today the school flourishes and is no longer taking in boarders, but some of those who did board here have some startling tales to tell, as do others who have worked or been taught here.

Included in the list of spooks, all sister's of the faith, are a nun who is seen inside the building (apparently she fell to her death from a staircase), a nun who is seen in the grounds, and a nun who died in her own bed on the third floor.

A lady called *Margaret who taught there briefly in 2005 says that some of the staff were aware of the school's reputation for being haunted, but being deeply religious and not believing in such things as ghosts, it appeared that most were reluctant to discuss the subject. Pupils from the school talk of the haunted cellars (although how this ties in with the hauntings reported seems unclear) and of a feeling of melancholy in some areas of the school. One pupil reported glasses inexplicably flying off the shelves in a chemistry lesson and others do say they have seen shadowy forms in the building itself. Reported stories of weeping statues of the Virgin Mary and door handles which rattle on their own all add to the mix.

There are lots of rumours about this place but there is a particularly amazing first hand account from an ex-boarder, a lady who was at the school from 1946 through to 1952. Christina Bedford now lives in Canada, but she was very keen to tell her story after years of keeping under wraps. She recalls that in those days the convent school was quite tough and, feeling homesick, she often cried herself to sleep. She remembered that on several occasions when she was this upset, she felt a gentle hand stroke the top of her head, until she eventually fell asleep. The nuns used to check the girls every night to make sure that they were asleep, and often they were not, so some of the girls used to pretend to be asleep and wait until the nuns had left the dormitory. Christina tells of one such night as she lay 'asleep', waiting for the nuns to finally leave, when she felt someone touch her foot. Afraid she had been found out, she quickly opened her eyes expecting to see one of the sisters rising above her. But there was no-one in the dormitory and as she stared quietly into the darkness and listened really intently she thought she heard singing, and then a candle appeared before her and seemed to float in space, disappearing almost as suddenly. She was afraid but she also felt comforted and in the end went off to sleep without waking anyone. She did try to tell some of the other girls of her experiences, but they scolded her for being so silly. As time went by, Christina learnt that the best policy was to keep this type of thing to herself.

Christina also felt as if she was being watched at certain times during the day, especially as she went through the Stations of the Cross (the Stations of the Cross are used as a meditative guide to prayer and are usually represented as a series of pictures or carvings portraying Christ's journey to the cross). She describes the feeling as ' ... someone watching over me', and in the end did mention this feeling to a kindly sister who told her that it was most likely Christina's own father who had died in 1942, just prior to her attending the convent school, and it was this comforting thought which kept her going. Nowadays, Christina is less sure as to who or exactly what this phenomenon was. But she also feels utterly convinced that spirits do exist and that one in some form or another had been there to look after her during her challenging time as a boarder.

*Name changed for reasons of anonymity

ROSSALL HALL, FLEETWOOD

Rossall Hall originated out of the estate of Rossall, wherein lay Rossall Grange, birthplace of Cardinal William Allen, founder of the Douai College, a seminary for recusant Catholic priests. Following the dissolution of the monasteries, the land was sold to Thomas Fleetwood in 1553 and at some time after Rossall Hall was built to replace the humble Rossall Grange. Subsequent members of both the Fleetwood and then the Hesketh family were in residence here for several hundred years thereafter. In fact, the town of Fleetwood, approximately eight miles outside of Blackpool, takes its name from its founder, Sir Peter Hesketh-Fleetwood, who was MP for Preston from 1832 to 1847. Rossall Hall evolved greatly over time and although much of its original fabric was damaged during a flood of 1833, the building you see today is more in the Victorian Gothic style of architecture and it remains a magnificent building in its own right.

In 1826, Sir Peter married Eliza Metcalf and they had several children together. Sadly, not one survived infancy and it is believed that Eliza, deeply distraught by the death of all her children, simply faded away herself in 1835. Rossall Hall became Rossall School in 1844, being founded by the Reverend Canon St Vincent Beechey and it seems that some time afterwards, ghostly encounters were being reported by pupils and staff alike. No wonder perhaps, as this once staunchly Catholic house gave itself up to become a Church of England school!

Ghostly sightings include that of a 'pallid lady' in the grounds of Rossall Hall, and of someone who also haunts the rooms and corridors of what was the old hall. There is some dispute over who this lady is. Some say she is the ill-fated Eliza, or Lady Fleetwood, as she became known. However, Peter Hough suggests in his book *Supernatural Lancashire* that according to the Jubilee History (published in 1895) it must have been an earlier Lady Fleetwood. The story goes that before Rossall Hall became a school in 1844 it was embroiled in some sort of smuggling racket, as contraband was brought up from the beach to the hall through tunnels running from the house to the beach area. It is alleged that a 'Lady Fleetwood' died in the tunnels beneath the hall after they collapsed whilst she was in them. How viable this is we cannot say with certainty, but there is no doubt that a ghostly feminine form is seen in both places – inside and out.

This pale, white lady patrols the grounds on one special day and night, that of Halloween, when the veil between the two worlds of the living and the dead seems to blur, just for a while, in order that we may communicate with our loved ones who have passed over.

Reported sitings of the white lady are rare these days and it seems that some are reluctant to talk about this unearthly visitation. However, it remains a well-known local legend and is thus worthy of a mention here.

ARNOLD SCHOOL, BLACKPOOL

The school was founded in 1896 by Frank Truswell Pennington and was originally called South Shore Collegiate School. It is believed to have been the site of an earlier Victorian school named Arnold House School and was named so after the headmaster of Rugby School, Dr Thomas Arnold. The ghost story retold here comes originally from Peter Underwood's excellent title *Ghosts of North West England* and although now almost thirty years old, the tale still has a grim fascination.

A young man named Peter Roscow was named as being head of an Occult Society which had been formed at the school during the late 1960s and early 1970s. The story goes that in 1970, following rumours that the school was haunted, Peter and eight members of the society sought permission from the headmaster to conduct a séance in the cellars of the old school building. All jolly hockey sticks you might think. However, Peter and his fellow paranormal enthusiasts got more than they bargained for, which probably goes some way to explaining why this type of thing would never be allowed to go on these days!

The boys apparently set up a makeshift Ouija board and made attempts to contact whoever or whatever they suspected was lurking there. Before long messages were being spelt out from a woman who told them that she had been murdered in 1854 by someone named Mercer. Apparently, she informed the hapless boys that she had been axed to death – a gruesome fate indeed. When she was questioned further as to why she was haunting the school, she replied 'For revenge'. When asked against who, she replied 'the law'. As if this was not enough, the boys asked for further evidence of her presence and almost immediately they reported an icy chill, despite being next to the boiler room. As some of the boys now began to feel quite unnerved by the whole experience, the séance was brought to a close, but not before they recited the Lord's Prayer for good measure. Even more strange, it is also reported that at the same time another group of boys was holding a séance in a classroom and they claimed to have made contact with a dead sailor, who had been hanged for murder. Could this have been the vengeful lady's axe killer? Whatever the truth, it is recorded that none of the boys knew beforehand that there was a local legend that former occupants of the headmaster's house had been hanged for murder.

A shocking tale by all accounts, but one which sadly cannot now be verified. It may be, however, that research back to the year of our poor lady's death could provide some answers ...

CHAPTER THREE

GHOSTS, GHOULS & GREASEPAINT

THE GRAND THEATRE, BLACKPOOL

Situated right in the heart of Blackpool's bustling town centre is the famous and historic Grand Theatre. Built in 1894, it was the brain-child of Thomas Sargenson, who for five previous summer seasons had staged a circus on the site. He commissioned renowned architect Frank Matcham to design this beautiful theatre and it remains a stunning example of the finest Victorian architecture.

As well as being a sumptuous testament to the architecture of the day, this theatre houses a secret: a ghostly spectre that haunts the upper circle balcony although is also often seen near the orchestra pit, where it is thought he met his untimely demise. Although no historic evidence can be found to say exactly who this 'phantom of the opera' is, it seems his legend is well known amongst locals and cast and crew who work within these haunted walls. Scores of actors, musicians, dancers and theatre goers have reported seeing his figure within the Grand Theatre. Stephen Mercer, the Marketing Manager who has worked at the Grand since 1999, has had numerous stories told to him by the many people who have passed though these doors. Stephen himself has not only heard strange noises and phantom footsteps, he has also felt and seen the presence of who everyone now believes is 'Charlie', a lovelorn suicide who threw himself off the upper circle balcony.

The story goes that in the 1930s during a staged performance that lasted three months (such was the norm in those days in terms of duration) a gentlemen suitor fell in love with an actress who was appearing there. This 'stage door Johnny' appeared daily after each performance in an effort to try to meet with her, but to no avail, as she rebuffed him at every turn. Still undeterred, for several months he continued to buy tickets for the show and always sat in the same seat in the front row of the upper circle. The story goes that eventually even he realised the futility of his quest and, in a last dramatic attempt to capture her attention, threw himself off the upper circle balcony one fateful and tragic night. From that time, 'Charlie' became the resident spirit at this now famous local theatre.

Stephen tells of an incident that happened seven years ago, where a lady thespian who was appearing there asked the ice cream seller, 'Do you have a ghost here? I can see a gentleman wearing unusual clothing, a flat cap, an old fashioned tweed suit and cravat seated in the upper circle, front row.' The same apparition was reported on a second night but this time Charlie was seen with two very fine Edwardian ladies wearing rather large, elaborate hats. Over many years he was seen again and the same apparition was reported to Stephen, who admits to having an interest in the paranormal, especially after so many stories were authenticated by so many different characters.

In 2006 a dancer in one of the shows was found sitting in the seat that has become 'Charlie's seat', along with two of her fellow cast members. When Stephen approached them and asked them how they were and what they were doing in the empty theatre seats, he was told that the dancer who was in Charlie's seat had asked her fellow dancers to come up to the upper circle with her, as she was convinced she had seen a man in old fashioned garb watching her rehearse on stage. So put off was she by him watching her that she went up to see who he was. The three girls found no-one of course, so they sat for a few moments pondering what had happened. As they sat there – the three dancers and now Stephen too– he told them the now famous story of Charlie. As they sat quietly in the upper circle, all of them heard loud footsteps overhead in the topmost balcony. The girls all let out a piercing shriek of fright and Stephen quickly looked up. He could see no-one. He ran up to the higher balcony where most of the lighting is housed and called out, but there was

nobody in this area. He left the girls, somewhat shaken, and went on an expedition around the entire theatre to find the source of the noise. He even considered that it may have been high jinks by one of the other cast members but no-one came forward to own up to this. He believes to this day that what they heard was not of this world; he is convinced this was not a prank.

He also tells of another incident of paranormal activity in the upper balcony area but not in 'Charlie's seat'. Often, Stephen pauses for a few minutes during his busy working schedule, to stop and sit a while during some of the performances staged there. He sits quietly at the back of the upper balcony in a particular seat if it is empty. As he sits there unnoticed at the back he has often felt someone very close to him, almost as if they are leaning in on him. He describes this feeling as unpleasant, likening it to when someone living inadvertently invades your personal space. He also complains that once or twice he has felt as if someone has touched the top of his head or ruffled his hair – this has been so noticeable as to make other staff ask him what he has been doing to his hair!

There are other reports of strange phenomena in another seat in the theatre. As well as people complaining that the seat feels 'cold', it also often feels damp, which is rather odd, as Stephen showed us where the air conditioning unit is and it is well off to the side of this seat. Downstairs in the stalls strong tobacco can be smelt sometimes , even though smoking is definitely not allowed in any public places these days. Stephen also reports seeing what he can only describe as a whiff of smoke appear in the vicinity of the orchestra pit and speculates that this is Charlie's departed soul trying to manifest itself where he met his dramatic death after falling from the balcony above.

Stephen also tells of the area on stage and behind it having an odd sense of presence. He has had cast members and crew complain to him that their props or equipment have been tampered with, or moved completely from one end of the stage to another, (it is an unwritten law of the theatre that no-one should ever touch the props!).

Stephen does now invite the general public into the theatre for late night vigils and it was on one of these such nights that local reporter Lisa Ettridge from Blackpool's *Evening Gazette* said she felt a peculiar sensation, as if someone was standing very close behind her seat. Later, as she sat in a seat at the front where Charlie would have thrown himself off, she complained of 'a weight on my shoulders as if somebody was pressing down'.

Stephen says he would love to be able to research exactly who 'Charlie' was but since the Grand has been through several changes of ownership, including at one time the multimedia company EMI, he now knows that many of the building's original archives are, sadly, lost for ever.

Whether the ghost or ghosts of the Grand are known to us or not, there is no doubt that something or someone haunts this regal theatre even today.

THE ROYAL PAVILION THEATRE, BLACKPOOL

After a feature in the *Evening Gazette* was published in mid 2008, appealing for local stories of ghostly encounters, Wilky Dee – a television personality and stage hypnotist for 40 years, contacted us to tell of his ghostly encounter at the Royal Pavilion theatre.

Wilky is well known in Blackpool for his 'Hypnotic Laughter Show' which played at a variety of entertainment venues in the town, and indeed all over the world, for many years. It was following a successful show at Gulliver's on Fleetwood promenade one stormy night, when the sea was pounding against the beach, that the seed was sown that would lead to his encounter with one of Blackpool's lesser known phantoms.

Sally Johnson, a producer and agent, had booked Wilky's stage show for one night at the venue, and she had thoroughly enjoyed the antics performed on stage by willing volunteers who were put under the hypnotic spell of Wilky's gaze. Accompanied by his assistant, Danielle, they had wowed the audience with an amusing school room routine, which involved a ghostly floating lamp stand. This was so successful that it frightened one volunteer so much he locked himself in the toilet! Little did they know that this pretence would soon be replaced with something far more sinister and frightening.

During the early 1990s, Sally booked the show for an entire summer season at the Royal Pavilion Theatre – a venue that had been used for many things over the years, including a public house, a revue bar, a cafeteria and a cinema.

Every Sunday night Wilky and Danielle would set up their props ready for an evening performance, but the season was doomed to fail from the start. Although Wilky's show was always popular, some of the other acts struggled to get punters through the box office. The season was cut short, and starting too soon in the year was the reason given.

It was one Sunday evening, after the show had finished and the audience had long gone, that Wilky was alone in the theatre, collecting up props and tidying up. As he walked across the silent stage, his attention was drawn to 'the gods' (a theatrical term to describe the highest balcony of seating), far above him. Access to that area had been boarded up and the doorway papered over many years earlier, as it was considered surplus to requirements and potentially unsafe with a very steep incline. But as he stood there, staring into the dark void, the distinct and brisk sound of footsteps walking along the balcony echoed around the theatre. He peered for several minutes, trying to see if there was anyone up there, but there was nothing to account for the strange sounds he had heard. Wilky decided to keep the inexplicable incident to himself and it wasn't until a few weeks later that he overheard someone else describing the same thing.

Mr Askham, the co-producer responsible for the summer season entertainment, was telling a colleague that he had heard footsteps coming from the deserted, and inaccessible, upper balcony. Sally had also heard it on another occasion, and Wilky added his tale to the now substantial list of spectral encounters. Talk of the theatre ghost was now a hot topic among theatre staff and performers, one of whom said he had felt distinctly eerie on a Sunday afternoon, before Wilky's show had arrived to set up; he suggested that the hypnotic elements of the performance may have woken a forgotten spirit from the past.

Soon afterwards, it came to light that when the building had been used as a revue bar a suicide had occurred in its environs, and a local paper had speculated that this might be the reason why a ghost, nicknamed 'Herbie', was haunting it. According to the story, which was related to the us by Wilky, a local Blackpool lad who worked as a driver had fallen head over heels in love with a young dancer who was working in the show. Each night, after he had finished work and the show had closed, he would drive up to the bar and pick up his girl, but one Sunday night he arrived earlier than usual and found her in a passionate embrace with a rival suitor. Distraught, he killed himself in a fit of rage.

Intrigued by this story, we delved a little deeper and discovered that prolific writer and undisputed 'King of Ghost Hunters' Peter Underwood had featured an account of this little-known ghost in his book *Ghosts of Northwest England* in 1978. Mr Underwood relates that in 1971 a séance was conducted inside the theatre by a medium named Terry Smith to try to ascertain who might be haunting the venue, after strange luminous lights and sounds had been reported. As the power

of the séance grew, and a deathly chill settled across the theatre, an entity communicated with the sitters and described himself as a driver of a horse-drawn vehicle. He said he was responsible for the haunting activity and he told a tale involving himself, a former doorman who wore a flower in his buttonhole, and an usherette. Despite the obvious differences in this version, it seems very likely that the 'spirit' of the story is that same known as Herbie.

At the end of the summer season Wilky's final curtain call signalled the end of the haunting, his hypnotic stage show sending the spirit off to finally rest in peace. According to Wilky, the ghost has never been heard since.

THE WINTER GARDENS, BLACKPOOL

The magnificent Winter Gardens complex was originally imagined as an indoor entertainment centre which could function just as easily during inclement weather conditions as on the sunniest summer day. Spanning a massive si-acre site, it opened to the public on July 11th 1878 offering a plethora of entertainment in its many halls, theatres and conservatories.

One of the most magical spaces in the complex has to be the Empress Ballroom, which was completed in the summer of 1896. It is one of the world's largest ballrooms, with floor space covering over 12,500 square feet. Its barrel-vaulted ceiling features elaborate plasterwork and is complimented by glittering chandeliers which create the decadent ambience of the past. Like its counterpart, the Tower Ballroom, which is also haunted, it has not been immune to the sensations of the spectral world ...

One of the strangest occurrences is the interference with the lighting systems which are controlled from a lighting desk. Stephen Mercer of Supernatural Events runs investigations for ghost enthusiasts and told us that he has experienced this curious phenomenon himself. The lights switching on and off again are combined with faint music and glimpses of shadows moving in the darker regions of the huge room.

According to Stephen the Empress Ballroom is just one area where ghosts lurk, and he told us that a spectral gentleman has also been reported walking around the main reception area late at night when the complex is about to close. The man apparently asks for directions out of the Winter Gardens but moments later disappears into thin air. His demeanour and tone suggest that he is from an era long gone and his appearances are accompanied by an icy chill which lingers long after he has gone.

CHAPTER FOUR

WINES & SPIRITS

THE SHIP & ROYAL INN, LYTHAM ST ANNES

The Ship & Royal on Lytham's Clifton Street has long been known as a haunted hotel, now a public house, and according to author Guy Lyon Playfair in his textbook of haunted hostelries, *The Haunted Pub Guide*, published in 1985, it is home to a tall spectral gentleman who has been spotted in the second floor grill room.

This spectre has been blamed in the past for rearranging paperwork and placing meat orders for the business, which had not been authorised, by telephone! Remarkable as it may seem, ghosts interfering with telephones, and even making calls themselves, is a common factor feature of many ghostly tales, and has been documented in countless cases throughout the history of psychic research.

An issue of the *Blackpool Gazette*, dating from 1978, tells the tale of a ghost nicknamed 'Charlie' by the management, but suggests the spirit is actually that of Squire John Talbot Clifton, a local who enjoyed spending time at the inn, and who died in Tenerife in 1928. Another copy of the same publication tells of a sighting years later, this time in 1983, and states that the ghost was seen on the second floor of the building.

Since moving into the half-derelict building in autumn 2007, Lee Jane and his girlfriend Gemma Rogers have experienced several visitations, thought to be the spirits of a mother and son who made a suicide pact at the beginning of the twentieth century, and who

drowned themselves in one of the building's upper floor bathrooms. The former hotel has twenty unused rooms which are out of bounds for health and safety reasons, and despite there being no plumbing in those rooms, the sound of running tap water is often heard in the dead of night.

So it seems 'Charlie' has been joined by a duo of spooks determined to frighten the new tenants. Late one night after the pub had closed for business, and staff members had finished cleaning up, the internal telephone rang. When it was answered there was nobody on the other end, and the office in which the other receiver is kept was fully locked up.

THE GRAPEVINE, POULTON-LE-FYLDE

In the historic Market Place of Poulton-le-Fylde is a run of terraced buildings housing, amongst other things, the Grapevine, a café by day and a restaurant and pub by night. Local historical sources tell us that this area once contained medieval timber framed cottages and a moot hall once stood at the end of this market place. In March 1732, however, all but the Grapevine escaped complete ruination after a fire broke out. Although this terrace was rebuilt, it did take several years of funding to replace the once-thriving businesses that were housed therein. In 1754 the first recorded business was that of John Hodgson, who opened up as a grocer and ironmonger in what is now the Grapevine. In the early 1750s, the market place became an area of mostly public houses and shops, once again serving the local community. We do not know if there were any deaths during this great fire, but local legend does speak of a woman who lost her life, though this cannot be proven. Either way, the hauntings reported recently date from only 40 years ago, coincidentally after a tragic unexplained death.

In 2002, the then owners of the Grapevine, which at that time was a pub, began to experience ghostly phenomena. Dave Nowell and his co-owner Karen Seddon reported to the local *Gazette* newspaper that they were experiencing 'odd happenings'. Glasses fell from shelves, literally flying through the air then dropping violently to the floor, doors opened and closed as if by some invisible hand and there were unexplained footsteps heard in many areas of the building when no-one was in the vicinity. Staff reported hearing a man's voice at times when no-one was in the premises and many experienced the unease of 'being watched'.

Several years passed and we can pick up the story again, as the next owner Jonathan Kozakiewicz also found the Grapevine to have an unusual aura all of its own. Jonathan bought the thriving business in 2005 and after major refurbishments opened up the middle floor

to this three-storey building and began to use it as a bar at night. It wasn't long before staff started to complain about some of the more unusual aspects of working here! As was reported by the previous owners, glasses frequently flew off the shelves of the bar and Jonathan himself was witness to such whilst operating the business on a day to day basis. He also told us of one particular incident on the ground floor, near to the cellar area, that to this day still baffles him. He told us that the previous owners had discovered a small room on the ground floor which seemed to have been boarded up and plaster boarded over. This box room seemed to be part of the next building along (number 17 and number 19 Market Place were at some point knocked together to form one business space) and Jonathan, during his refurbishment project, fashioned this almost purpose-built space into the disabled toilet.

One very busy weekend not long after he had opened, he was working on the ground floor meeting and greeting customers and generally keeping a beady eye on things. At one point he passed by the newly fashioned toilet and noted that it was shut. Some minutes later, he passed by the toilet again and saw it was still closed, so he carefully knocked to ascertain if anyone was inside. There was no response. Tactfully, he stood silently by the door, waiting for them to come out, wondering what on earth they were up to. After some time, which he describes as an inordinately long period, he again knocked and this time called out. Again, no reply, but this time, fearing someone may be in difficulties inside, he tried the door handle, which remained firm against his grip. Unable to open the door, he now feared the worst, which was that he was going to have to break into the toilet to effect a 'rescue' of kinds. He stood and tried that door handle for several minutes more and then, exasperated, stood back to consider his next plan of action, naturally fearing what he might find inside! At this moment, the door simply and silently swung open towards him and he admits now that he almost jumped out of his skin, not only because

he wasn't expecting anyone to open it, but because to his horror there was no-one inside.

Jonathan has never quite got over this experience as he says he has never had anything like it happen to him before or since. As incredible as it sounds he still tried to think logically about whether he would need to have this door fixed, so he attempted to shut and then re-open the door himself. It both closed and opened perfectly, without a hitch, leaving him bewildered and in the end, believing that he had experienced some sort of ghostly encounter, the likes of which his staff had been reporting to him for weeks. Ever the sceptic, he told us he still had his father look at this door the very next day, in case he had been imagining it and there was indeed something wrong with the fastening or lock on the door. Of course, the reality is that he didn't find anything wrong with the door and although this never happened again – at least not to Jonathan – he did relate another story which involved one of his managers who worked alongside him called Peter. Peter was the assistant manager of the business and as such had to open up and close down the premises each morning and night, depending on his shift. One night, Jonathan, who lives close by, was standing opposite the Grapevine waiting for Peter to open up. It was a winter's evening and although quite early it was beginning to get dark. However, according to Jonathan there was sufficient street lighting for him to watch Peter go in and open up as normal. Within minutes, his mobile phone rang and it was Peter, telling him to come quickly as he suspected the pub had intruders. Jonathan rushed across the square just as Peter was coming out, locking the door again rather shakily. 'Someone's inside', he said, 'but don't worry, I've locked them in.' They stood for a moment discussing whether or not to inform the police. The fact that the police station is only opposite the pub, however, gave them confidence to go in themselves and investigate. Upon doing so, however, they discovered no intruder and in fact nothing out of the ordinary. Jonathan insisted Peter tell him why he thought there was someone rifling through the place and was told, 'but I definitely saw someone in there as I opened up ... I know I did!'

Such occurrences soon came to be accepted as part and parcel of owning the Grapevine and it wasn't long before Jonathan had to put up with staff and customers telling him what they had seen or heard

in the way of ghostly sightings. One customer, a gentleman who went
to use the gents toilets, came back 'ashen-faced', as Jonathan describes
him and told him he was sure he had see a woman's face staring back
at him, in the toilet mirror. He was naturally quite shaken by such,
no less when he realised it wasn't any living lady who had ventured in
there by mistake, but what he believed to be a ghost. Debbie, Jonathan's
mother, frequently helped out in the business and at first was highly
sceptical of the whole affair, although she admits that so many of the
staff told her the same types of things that she began to believe that
there was something to this ghost story after all. She recalls a time
when she was in the kitchen upstairs alone when she heard the chef's
buzzer go off (a device they had set up to let staff know when the food
was ready to be collected from the kitchen above to be taken to the
restaurant below) when she was the only person in the kitchen and
had not touched the buzzer. Debbie also recalls the distinct feeling of
'not being alone', especially in the early mornings when opening up
to clean the premises. She too had a distinct dislike of the gents' and
disabled toilets, which had nothing to do with the cleaning of them.

As Jonathan passed the ownership on to newcomers Abigail and
Darren Woodcock in January 2008, it wasn't long before they too
began to feel the spirit of the place! Abigail remains quite sceptical,
up to a point, as she cannot escape the general feeling of apprehension
that she herself often feels whilst working in the building late at night
when customers and staff have gone home. Abigail says she has been
told by customers who have frequented the establishment for some
decades that there is most definitely a ghostly presence in the building.
Her staff often report hearing ghostly footsteps on the approach to the
attic which now houses the kitchen, only to open the door to find that
no-one is there. Head Chef Suzanne Stuttle often senses that she is
being watched in her kitchen and feels that someone is standing too
close to her, close enough to feel their breath on her neck. She often
hears thumps and thuds on the wall just outside the kitchen and again,
upon opening her door, finds that there is no living soul around. Other
staff members working in the kitchen have even reported having
chestnuts thrown at them, an oddity in itself as this is not something
which is, or has ever been, on their menu! Another story told by
Abigail involves another member of staff, Barbara Woolford, who was

loading crockery and glasses into the dumb waiter. All the staff are aware that this equipment will not work properly if you do not close the doors. One day, as they waited for the pots to come back down from the attic area close to the kitchen, they realised that it had got stuck. Annoyed, Barbara marched upstairs to see what the problem was, only to find the doors wide open, thus rendering the dumb waiter inoperable. She ran back down the stairs white-faced according to Abigail, and flatly refused to go into the kitchen for some months after, until she had plucked up the courage. Debbie also confirms this story as all of them had worked together under her and Jonathan's ownership. Debbie herself recalls many incidents with the infamous dumb waiter and although she insists that she too would shut it firmly, it often failed to move because it had been miraculously opened up again by an unseen hand.

Lily Isherwood has been with the Grapevine for over three years and has worked alongside both past and present owners. She describes hot and cold spots in the building, and near the coffee machine she and Abigail both describe what feels like a cobweb wafting across your face. When they put their hands to their face there is in fact nothing there, no real cobweb. This is described by the pair as feeling as if you have really 'walked into something' and is described by all as most disconcerting. Lily is a sensible type who says that although she is often quite sensitive to such things, she would only ever report what she knows to be true in terms of what she has actually seen, heard or felt herself. No-one seems certain who or what is haunting the Grapevine but many believe it could be the spirit of a tragic death by suicide which occurred here in the 1960s in the gun store (which was once housed next door to the Grapevine).

Both Abigail and the Jonathan, say that it is common knowledge that a local man, named Freddy Smith*, shot himself. Several other locals, still alive today, recall this man well and speak kindly of him and remember with sadness the circumstances of his death.

Lily tells us that she is not averse to giving 'Freddy', as he is affectionately known, a good talking to in the early mornings as she cleans up, telling him, 'Now, no nonsense today please Freddy, there's too much to do!'

All the staff and owners you talk to here – past and present
– do believe that there is something haunting this ancient building.
Whether it is our very own Freddy, or some other poor lost soul who
lingers here still, no-one can be really sure. What we do know is that
all the staff and customers have known for some time about the 'ghost
of the Grapevine', and although it is not malevolent in any way, it
certainly can spook you – day or night!

* Name has been changed to protect identity

THE SHARD RIVERSIDE INN, HAMBLETON

It is not unusual to hear stories of animal hauntings. Our beloved
pets often form strong attachments to us, and we to them. After
their demise, they may still linger in their homes or favourite walking
places, re-living moments of kindness – perhaps on the look-out for
their owner. At the Shard Riverside Inn, it is a faithful dog that haunts
this local hostelry, as might most often be expected in such tales.

The earliest account of the haunting is found in Graham Evans,
1989 book *Places, Legends and Tales of The Fylde.* In it, he tells of a
barmaid who was opening up early one winter's night, just as dusk was
beginning to descend. She turned the key in the door and entered the
inn and was shocked to see a black and white dog dart across the floor
of the bar and run into the adjoining room. As she knew there were no
dog owners on the premises at this time, and in fact the pub had not
yet been opened up to the public, she quickly scurried after it to shoo
it out. She could, however, find no trace of the dog in the next room, or
indeed anywhere else on the premises. Customers, locals particularly,
often used to ask, 'Whose is the little black and white dog sitting over
there in the corner?' – only to look again and see no dog at all.

The current owners of the Shard Inn, the Hurst family, have run it
since 1999. Paul Hurst told us that there is a well-known local legend
about the inn being haunted by the ghost dog and although he himself
has never seen it, Paul recalls that the previous owner, George, saw the
phantom hound himself and did tell him about it when they took over
the running of the inn. Since that time, new customers who visit the
pub, come to the bar and ask for a bowl of water for the 'cute little

black and white dog outside'. Staff have become so used to this request that they now urge the person to go back outside and see if the dog is still there – of course, the dog has vanished. These same people are then told, 'Don't worry, it isn't a stray that's just wandered off again, its our little ghost dog!'

Paul has had several overnight guests tell him they were aware of a dog whimpering outside their bedrooms throughout the night, often getting up (quite annoyed sometimes!), opening the bedroom door expecting to see the pesky pooch, only to find that of course there is no dog there at all. Previous sightings of the little dog have been mostly in the downstairs areas. However, these newly appointed rooms on the first floor have only been open to the public in the last three years, so Mr Hurst speculates that this is why these reports are becoming more frequent upstairs, where it is most likely the original bedrooms to the old house were. Prior to these new rooms being let no-none lived on the premises nor stayed overnight.

But could there be another phantom here too, not of the canine variety? The current owner remembers too a local lady who hailed from Knott End and was their cleaner some years back. She regularly complained of the feeling that she was being watched and claimed that things got thrown around at her in the pub whilst she was trying to work. Ashtrays mysteriously shot off tables, beer mats flew through the air just missing her and ornaments dotted around the bar moved from their usual place, to reappear somewhere else completely random. Sadly, Paul recalls, she didn't remain with the family for very long after these episodes!

This phantom hound seems well known and everyone who lives locally has heard of the events which surround this ghost story, as it is both unusual and heartbreaking. Extraordinary heroics such as a dog saving its owners life, only to lose theirs in the endeavour, are not unique. However, this story is different in as much as it was the owner who died trying to save his beloved pooch, and not vice versa.

In the 1960s, the local newspaper ran a 'human interest story' pertaining to this mystery surrounding the ghost dog, which went back to 1908. The story followed the sad demise of a Mr Norman Renshaw, son of wealthy James and Mary Renshaw who resided at the very grand house known as Shard House, nestled on the banks of the Wyre estuary. Norman Renshaw was at that time a young man about town, he enjoyed all the trappings of his parent's success and he followed the pursuits of any Edwardian gentlemen of his time. He loved to ride his horses and was the proud owner of a new motor boat, and he often took his faithful black and white mongrel dog Jack walking along the river bank close to his home. The two obviously had a strong bond so when Jack fell from the new boat into the river and began to struggle in the strong currents, Norman jumped in to save him. Sadly, Jack survived his swim but brave owner Norman did not. On Friday 14th August 1908, that Norman, only 25 years of age, lost his life attempting to save the little dog, who had fallen from the new boat into the River Wyre and was struggling to swim against the strong current of this tidal tributary.

Little Jack lived for many years with the Renshaws, but tragedy was never far away as Norman's father also died just three years later – perhaps he never quite recovered from the tragedy of his son's death. Jack died of old age in January 1915 and was buried along with another favourite dog called Prinnie who died later that same year. As a testament to the heroic action of her son and to the dog he loved so much, Mary Renshaw erected a gravestone, now located in the car park area of the Shard Inn, which marks where faithful Jack was buried. The inscription reads, 'In affectionate memory of my dear son's dog Jack. Died January 15th 1915. His master lost his life in saving this dumb faithful friend in the year 1908 M.A.C.R. Also of dear little Prinnie, who died August 27th 1915. Faithful unto the last.'

Mary died here alone in 1943. On her death, Mary and her family were together again, all three buried in Hambleton cemetery beneath a magnificent carved stone piece entitled 'Reunited'. Poor little Jack seems still drawn to this place, once his home and where he enjoyed many a happy day walking along the river bank with his owner and friend, Norman. This is a story which moves all those who hear it and it comes as no surprise to many that it is this devoted dog that now haunts his master's former home – perhaps searching for him even now, in an effort to be 'reunited' himself.

THE EAGLE & CHILD PUBLIC HOUSE, WEETON

For those ghost hunters who are looking for a country diversion away from the main hub of Blackpool town, the Eagle & Child on Singleton Road at Weeton can provide a warming welcome with some spooky charm.

The building is one of the oldest public houses in the North West and was built in 1585, taking its name from the family crest of Lord Derby, who once owned many of the surrounding lands, and whose spectre haunted the grounds of former Mowbreck Hall (see page 63).

The building is a quaint inn full of character and is allegedly one of the resting places of Oliver Cromwell during the Civil War. Secret passages are said to run from the cellar rooms to allow people to evade

capture if the authorities arrived unannounced. Some interesting artefacts can be seen by inquisitive visitors, including the door handle of a spice cupboard from 1695, an ancient sword discovered during renovations and a set of mounting steps from 1755.

The ghost, which is now accepted as simply part of the fabric of the building, is known locally as 'Bleeding Ears Murph', and it is said that after the stroke of midnight his spirit manifests in the bar to scare away customers. Although the phantom has never been seen, he is heard chattering away incessantly through the night. According to one account, he is the ghost of a former highwayman who, after felling from London, ended up here to escape punishment for his crimes.

THE FOXHALL PUBLIC HOUSE, BLACKPOOL

Edward Tyldesley is believed to have built the first Fox Hall at some time towards the end of the 17th century and it is mentioned in the *Victoria County History* publication of 1912 as being ' … a mansion of the Tyldesleys of Myerscough.' The name Fox Hall is said to be taken from the Tyldesley penchant for keeping foxes and is recorded in Thomas Tyldesley's diary of 1713 thus: 4th June 1713 –...gave 2s.6d. pro a ffox cub'.

As odd as this seems, the original name of Fox Hall has stuck, and today this place is an established public house and hotel to which thousands of holiday makers flock every year. Of course the current building you see bears no resemblance to its original form, when it was described in Fishwick's *The History of the Parish of Bispham in the County of Lancaster* [1887] as: … 'a small three-gabled building, with a small tower at one side of it. The walls were made of sea-shore cobble stones, and were of great thickness.' During the first Jacobite rebellion of 1715, Fox Hall was also a haven for Popish recusants. At some time in the 1860s, sadly, the old hall was demolished.

Local residents report sightings of priests dressed in their familiar robes, both in and around the vicinity of the old Foxhall. The newer red-bricked building replaced an older one which over the years spread in size from a much humbler structure to its present location on the corner of the promenade and Tyldesley Road. Ted, a Fleetwood man,

tells of a friend who worked there during the late 1980s, before the red brick frontage was refurbished, who whilst on duty stocking up the bar began to feel as if he was being watched by some unseen presence. This feeling continued for about 15 minutes, after which point the temperature dropped remarkably, culminating in an icy draft behind him. As the cold air shifted away from him, he looked intently towards one end of the bar and saw a 'monk-like figure in brown sackcloth robes' drifting through the wall in one corner of the room. As if this wasn't bad enough, some months later he and another member of staff also reported seeing a solid-shaped, scruffy looking individual in knee breeches and rough cloth shirt. When they called out to him, he quite literally vanished like a puff of cigarette smoke, dissipating into the air around them. There are reported sightings of smugglers here, so we could perhaps theorise that this was such an individual returning to his favourite haunt!

Foxhall now is a dance club and bar called the Reflex but whoever still lurks within these new walls plainly still feels some allegiance to the old hall, as even the loud music and hundreds of revellers have not deterred this spirit from making a guest appearance every now and then.

The Lobster Pot, Blackpool

The Old Lobster Pot, as it was called, was once a fine restaurant before becoming a nightclub in the 1970s, which many locals frequented. Now, the site houses both the Superbowl and Brannigans bar and nightclub. At one time, access to the Lobster Pot was from Market Street only, but now access is also from the promenade.

Edith Finlayson, a local lady of 76 years young, worked at these premises from 1965–66 when it was a restaurant. Upon commencing work there, she heard stories from the other staff members about their resident ghost. Being a staunch no-nonsense type of Scottish woman, she took these stories with a very large pinch of salt – initially!

Edith worked in what was a storeroom next to the kitchen and it was from here that the chefs would come to collect their food from the pantry and fridges for the night ahead. She also helped wait on during busy periods. Although she worked there only for a relatively short time, she heard of and experienced several, what she terms 'oddities'. Dark shadowy shapes were seen by all the staff in this area and many reported a sense of being watched. Several of Edith's work colleagues, who were young, attractive girls, had the experience of being playfully pinched, both on the arm or, more disconcertingly, on the bottom, as they went about their work! This 'pinching' ghost was seen more as a bit of a nuisance, rather than a malicious presence. Whatever his motivation, the staff did label him as a 'bit of a lad'. That said, it was Edith who felt another a side of this ghost, a side which she found increasingly unnerving. Edith said that although she never felt (physically) anything herself, the storeroom where she worked had a particularly unpleasant atmosphere of its own and she often felt 'spooked' working there alone. So much so that she would try to organise her shifts so that she would not have to work alone in there, even when the restaurant was open and paying customers were in. In the end, she disliked working there so much that she left to work elsewhere, despite the wage being quite good for the time.

Years later, when the Lobster Pot became the Superbowl, inexplicable things began to happen in the floor above which houses the bowling alleys, including equipment that works the ball release for the bowling beginning to work on its own. Often, staff locking up late at night heard bowls being hurled along the lanes, only to go back and discover nothing 'out of the ordinary' at all and no-one there. Other phenomena include alarms going off at night when no-one was in the building, and the shape of a man being seen in the bar area after hours when all the customers had gone home.

This is another one of those hauntings which is well known locally, and yet who this ghost actually is may be harder to determine. There is a rumour that the ghost is a chef who committed suicide in the building during the 1960s, but details are sketchy and, to date, despite research, his true identity remains a mystery. Whoever he is, if this 'bowling ghost' is also the 'pinching ghost', one wonders whether in between terrorising the ladies, he enjoys a game of bowls …

THE OLD COACH HOUSE HOTEL, BLACKPOOL

Just off the seafront in the South Shore district of Blackpool, the discerning visitor seeking overnight accommodation might find themselves outside the Old Coach House Hotel on Dean Street. According to the hotel's website, the building is the oldest remaining house in the area and certainly stands out, with its striking black and white timber mock-Tudor façade, landscaped gardens and stunning conservatory.

This award-winning hotel retains the aura of times past; wooden four-poster beds and ancient stone fireplaces create a charm which is rare in a town over filled with 'run of the mill' establishments. But the Old Coach House Hotel not only offers first class accommodation, it also serves 'haunt' cuisine!

The dining room is home to a pair of harmless haunts who have been glimpsed observing diners as they enjoy a tasty treat. The first has affectionately been named 'Shirley', a ghostly lady of unknown origin whose activities seem to focus on looking after the room and its guests. The second is a more severe spirit, that of a hungry man who stares intently at his living counterparts from the shadows. Witnesses describe him wearing a black cap and cloak and have suggested that he might be in need of one of the hotel's delicious meals himself!

THE BOAR'S HEAD INN, GREAT MARTON

The Boar's Head, on Preston Old Road in Marton, is a modern public house with a contemporary appearance, not exactly the kind of place you might expect supernatural happenings to take place, but it was at the centre of an outburst of supernatural activity in 2008 when Landlady Tracy Mappley first encountered the activity of the building's ghosts.

The *Blackpool Gazette* followed the story as part of their 'Fylde's Most Haunted' series of tales from the district by reporter Julia Bennett, who described the following account in her copy:

> It began when Mrs Mappley started to hear strange sounds during the dark hours; banging and tapping noises which despite investigation, could not be explained. After checking that no-one had been locked inside the

building by mistake, she returned to her bedroom shouting out "whatever you're doing, stop it now" at which point the sounds abruptly ceased.

The activity continued with noticeable drops in temperature and the sensation of sickness in certain parts of the building. The distinct, and unnerving, feeling that she was not alone, and that a 'presence' pervaded the otherwise peaceful atmosphere of the place, began to concern her and she decided to seek help when her jewellery began disappearing without any natural explanation.

Tracy contacted a team of local paranormal investigators and asked them to undertake an investigation to ascertain what, or who, might be haunting the pub. After setting up their equipment the team conducted a séance, using a medium to make contact with any wandering spirits which were present; during the sitting tables moved of their own accord and information was received which explained the activity was being caused by the presence of a small child named 'Sean' who had passed to the spirit world in 1855. This mischievous entity was intent on causing mischief, rather than trying to inflict fear upon those who encountered it.

Following the paranormal investigator's visit, Tracy's attitude toward her ghostly guest changed now she knows who it is and that it means her no harm she is happy to live side by side with it. She told the *Gazette* 'I definitely believe now, it doesn't bother me though. I suppose it's just having a bit of a laugh.'

A second spirit, of the supernatural kind, is said to haunt this friendly public house, and he is thought to be the ghost of a former local farmer named George who, despite passing away in 1838, still visits his favourite old drinking haunt to raise a glass with the living!

Frenchman's Cove Bar & Bistro, Blackpool

Situated on South King Street in the heart of haunted Blackpool lies the themed bistro and bar Frenchman's Cove. The menu, which according to the *Blackpool Gazette*, once featured zebra, camel and reindeer, is strange enough, but that is nothing compared to the peculiar ghostly goings on in the cellar below ...

Before the bar opened to the public, owner Billy Johnson explained that after five different contractors had been booked to carry out work on the building, they had all reported the same uncanny feeling of being watched in the cellar.

At first he dismissed the idea that the area might have a spectral resident, but after investigating the cellar himself he agreed that the sensation of being accompanied by an unseen presence was certainly tangible. The building once housed Duckworth's Tobacco Warehouse – perhaps the lingering spirit dates from this previous architectural incarnation?

Determined to rid the place of the residual traces of former phantoms, he vowed to have the building exorcised, saying the only spirits on the menu should be those served in glasses! Whether or not the exorcism actually took place is unknown, but one source states that staff working late at night still have a sense that they are not alone ...

THE VICTORIA PUBLIC HOUSE, FLEETWOOD

The Victoria public house on Dock Street, is one of Fleetwood's oldest pubs. It was built in 1836 as part of the development of the new town of Fleetwood, under the direction of Sir Peter Hesketh-Fleetwood who founded the town in the same year.

Mr Eric Pollitt, who is the current leaseholder and owner of the brewery Brewberry Inns Ltd has become quite concerned as several bizarre things have come to light recently involving both staff and clientele. Terrified bar staff have reported seeing what they described as a 'mysterious figure' – a male wearing slightly outdated black clothing and an old fashioned style white shirt – standing near an old original fireplace. His sudden appearance and subsequent disappearance, right in front of their eyes, has made many of them nervous to work in the pub late at night or on their own. Barman Chris Boehme reported to the local newspaper that he has seen door handles jerking up and down, as if someone is trying to come into one of the rooms there. As he investigated to see if there really was anybody on the other side struggling to open the door perhaps, he was shocked to find no-one there at all. He has also been witness to loud banging and uncanny footsteps coming from overhead in one of the rooms upstairs whilst he has been working in the bar. Again, these bangs and phantom wanderings have been found to be from no-one living, as the rooms in question above the bar were completely empty.

In desperation, Mr Pollitt decided to enlist the help of local clairvoyant Polly Stephenson, in an attempt to investigate the hauntings there and possibly help unravel the mystery of the 'man in black'. Polly got more than she bargained for as she had the misfortune to experience the ghostly presence trying to take her over. This type of spirit possession can often happen where a sensitive or medium will allow the departed spirit to communicate through them by using their body – voice, arms and legs etc. – but it can have its pitfalls and is considered by some to be dangerous if the sensitive or medium is not experienced in such things. Polly herself described feeling as if she was changing physically into a much larger person – that of a well-built man. She also noticed (as did others around her) that her voice became distinctly masculine and deeper as she felt his continued presence trying hard to invade her body. She also saw during this trance-like state a horse and some old barrels appear in the pub and went on to describe other aspects of the surroundings which she appeared to be seeing through his eyes. Candles which were lit during this session were blown out vigorously when asked if the ghost could give some proof that it was present in the room. Knocks, banging and tapping sounds were also heard in response to questions asked.

Mr Pollitt remains quite sceptical but he accepts that many other people have seen or felt something, and mediums who have come into the pub have all experienced some form of contact with this departed soul. To this day Mr Pollitt still does not know exactly who it is that haunts his pub – perhaps this unobtrusive spirit does not know that time has been called!

Raikes Hall, Blackpool

Raikes Hall has a chequered past. There has been a dwelling of some sort on the site for many centuries and it is recorded that Mr William Hornby, born in 1761, bought the Raikes Hall estate shortly before his death in 1824. He bequeathed it on his death to his youngest brother John, and the sisters of the Society of the Holy Child Jesus took a lease on the hall in 1859. What a desolate place this must have been back then, as this area, almost 40 acres in total, was surrounded only by fields. By 1871 it had fallen into private ownership and from very humble beginnings, it grew in stature to become a hugely popular entertainment complex. Raikes Hall Gardens, as it was known, featured circus entertainment, lavish gardens, a boating lake, a theatre and later even housed within its expansive grounds Blackpool FC.

By the end of the century Raikes Hall Gardens began to lose its appeal, despite its many fantastic attractions, due to the ever increasing competition from the seafront attractions. In 1901 the land and the old hall were sold off in lots, and the once famous hall became licensed premises, which is how it stands today. Today the Raikes Hall public house is all that remains of the garden and visitor's attraction and these days is more known for its ghostly rather than human visitors.

A local resident named Mary* describes her experience one 'quiet' night in the pub in the winter of 2007. She had gone in to meet friends there and enjoy the live music and as she sat waiting for her friends to arrive she saw quite distinctly the form of a lady in nun's habit, head covered, rosary beads swinging from her neck, walking with some urgency from one room into the next. She laughed out loud thinking that this was the band in some form of crazy garb, and as she ordered her next drink at the bar she asked one of the bar staff which band

was appearing tonight and whether they were in costume. The staff member replied that this was a local jazz band and, no, they didn't wear costumes! As they got deeper into conversation, Mary told him what she had seen. The barman looked remarkably unconcerned as he retorted, 'Oh, that'll be our ghost nun you've just seen then!', as he continued to pull his pint. Mary, to this day, cannot believe how clearly she saw this figure, how life-like and how normal in appearance she seemed. She says that this is not how she ever imagined her very first sighting of a ghost would be. She had always believed that the prerequisite for seeing a ghost was the expected sudden chill, malevolent atmosphere and the like. In fact, she describes the opposite feeling during her encounter – one of almost friendly familiarity, nonchalance and serenity. So much so that it certainly did not stop her frequenting the pub again.

The Nun of Raikes Hall is well documented locally and many have seen her, or indeed heard her, in various parts of the pub. There are also reports of strange noises emanating from the cellars, which no-one relishes investigating after dark! Actual first-hand accounts of this well-known haunting are sketchy in terms of when it all might have started, but it is generally believed that this manifestation of a nun seen here may date back to those times when the nuns were in residence. The legend goes that a nun was drowned in the sea nearby, although it must be said that the sea is actually some miles from the pub's current position. It is alleged that she travels back to this, her 'home' and as well as apparently taking delight in being seen in general, and she has a penchant for moving objects around in the pub. She also appears to enjoy the in-house Jazz band!

*assumed name

CHAPTER FIVE

GRAND OLD HAUNTS

WINDMILL COTTAGE, PREESALL

Preesall, situated approximately 20 miles out of Blackpool, is mentioned in the Doomsday Book and the name comes from the Viking word meaning 'the hill and the heath'. Today, you can still see the remains of an historic windmill in Park Lane, Preesall, which was actually used for woodworking and not grinding corn or wheat. Very close to this windmill lies an old cottage, which may originally have had some links with the mill, (possibly as a workers cottage), during some time in its history. *Windmill Cottage is believed to date from c.1650, although the exact date seems uncertain as deeds only go back as far as the mid 1800s. This is a long way out of the main hub of the bright lights of Blackpool, but there is a most interesting ghost story connected with the building, which could not go unmentioned in this book.

Several local people know of the hauntings in this cottage and the facts surrounding the current owners, *Sheila and Brian Smithall, who have lived here since 1971. Sheila is a lovely lady, now in her 80s, and whilst not in the greatest health is still an extremely vibrant and fascinating woman. She wrote a book and had it published herself diarising the events of her life in Windmill Cottage, and it includes details of the full 'hands on' restoration of this old worker's cottage and, more importantly for us, its many ghosts. Sheila's stories are numerous and these paranormal activities seem to occur with alarming frequency, and we were privy to some ourselves whilst we were with her on the day she showed us around her home.

The first poltergeist activity she recorded began in 1972, as she was well under way with the 'knocking about of her new home', (as she herself puts it). She and Brian had been repairing some of the cobblestone walls within the house, and as they went along they stored the cobbles on land to one side of the cottage, in order to use them later to rebuild the walls with natural and reclaimed materials. One day Sheila was alerted to a tremendous crashing thud which seemed to have come from the front door, itself an ancient piece of wood and ironwork which still stands intact to this day. She went to the door, not quite knowing what to expect, and as she opened it, she found a huge boulder of cobblestone, 'the size of a cannon ball'. She noticed that the front door was slightly dented and scratched, suggesting that the stone had been hurled against the door and she was initially alarmed, suspecting vandals or children playing pranks. To her amazement, as she went to remove this missile she found it did indeed resemble a cannon ball and she was quite unable to lift it herself (bear in mind this was over 30 years ago and Shelia was in those days fit and no stranger to hard physical labour). She had no alternative but to await Brian's return from work, when the two of them then struggled to move it from the doorstep and laid it in the garden, some good distance from the house. Although this seemed almost unexplainable, it was, at that time, an isolated incident, so Sheila though little of it – until a few months later.

That same year was the first time that Sheila had her first witness to the paranormal activities she had been living with daily. Her neighbour Betty had called in for a coffee and as they sat chatting away, she jumped and said, 'I've just seen someone going up your stairs!' As they were alone in the house, she asked her neighbour to describe the clothes that they were wearing and was astounded to be told: 'they had on a sort of long garment, slightly open at the front but with another garment underneath it and a cord was hanging from the waist, like the habits that monks used to wear.' They both sat silently for a moment and then to their surprise, both saw what they described as a wisp of smoke wafting down the stairs and then disappearing through a wall into another room. Sheila recalls in her book that the neighbour said she would never 'if you paid me' live in this cottage as it gave her the creeps. Sheila said that although they remained firm friends, Betty never did call round again for coffee, or anything else for that matter!

Another witness to these disturbing events was one of Sheila's daughters Tracy, who describes how, one night in 1976 at around two in the morning, she was tossing and turning and listening to the grandfather clock downstairs – tick, tock, chime when she turned over in her bed to see a strange shape, whitish in hue and only about three feet high (she later estimated) dart across the room. As she stared terrified at the shape which had now moved to the adjoining bedroom door leading to her eldest sister's bedroom, the 'thing' seemed to grow in height until it was as tall as the ceiling and its mass then turned to look at her, then melted away into nothing and the darkness took over the space where it had been. On another night in the same bedroom Tracy was awoken by her bed being lifted off the floor, and then dropped again heavily enough to make a huge thud. She literally leapt from the bed to the light switch and turned on the light. Closer examination of the bed showed that the castors were still in place and she found that she could not explain what had occurred. Sleep did not come easily that night.

It wasn't long before even Brian had to own up to the fact that perhaps there was something in their cosy cottage which shouldn't be there. One day he was off work and ill in bed with flu, and as he drifted in and out of recuperative sleep, he thought he heard someone's voice. Thinking it must be either his wife returning home early from work or his daughters back from school, he looked at the clock, which read 12 noon. There shouldn't have been anyone home at this time of day so he listened intently as the sounds intensified until he could recognise it as a girl's voice singing a lullaby. He was sure this singing was coming from his daughter's bedroom, so this time he called out to her several times, with no response. The sound seemed to become louder and clearer and in the end he struggled out of bed, annoyed by now, and flung open her bedroom door: the singing stopped and despite his searching the cottage (as ill as he felt) there was, of course, no-one home – not in the real sense, at least!

Another notable experience occurred during that same year and one which Sheila recalls with some satisfaction as, once again, she felt she had a witness to events here. She was doing the housework one

Sunday alone in the cottage, as Brian and her daughters were out for the day. After several hours of intensive cleaning, she took a tea break outside in the garden and relaxed for 10 minutes or so. As she sat there enjoying the peace and tranquillity, she glanced up at the window to the back of the property. She observed the curtain wafting in what she thought was the breeze, but then strained her eyes harder to see that the curtain was in fact being held back by a hand. Alarmed, she sat up, looking more intently, and was amazed to see the face of an old woman peering back at her through the glass. She could see the old lady's face quite clearly and she described her as being approximately eighty years old, wrinkled in her face and with a black mop cap on her head, tied under the chin with a ribbon of the same colour. Around her shoulders she clutched a shawl with her other hand, the shawl being fastened across her front with some sort of fancy brooch. Their eyes locked and for a moment seemed to stare each other out, and then quickly Sheila gathered her wits about her, leapt from her resting place and ran up the stairs as fast as she could. On entering the room where she had seen the old lady, she found nothing. She tells us she did search the house, fearing that someone had wandered in, though in her heart of hearts she already knew this was unlikely and that what had just happened was all part and parcel of living at Windmill Cottage.

The story doesn't end here however. Whilst working in her shop several weeks later, a visitor to the area remarked upon the card on the door of the shop which gave the name and address of her as the proprietor. The woman was astounded: 'What a coincidence,' she cried, 'I was brought up at Windmill Cottage over forty years ago – my father was the head gardener to the big house next door.' Naturally Sheila was keen to chat to this lady, hoping she would perhaps be able to tell her more about the old place and its former inhabitants. Sheila described the renovation work and all the ghostly phenomena she had experienced over the years, to which the visitor replied, 'What a load of nonsense ... I never saw nor heard anything out of the ordinary in all the times we were there.' She then went on to explain that in her opinion the only really 'odd' thing was a great aunt of her father's named Mariah. Apparently she came to stay on several occasions and loved the cottage dearly. She was always given the bedroom at the back of the house, the one facing the garden.

The visitor described this lady as an eccentric, having a penchant for dressing in the garb of an old Victorian lady, not her era at all, of course. When pushed to describe exactly how the aunt dressed the visitor replied: 'She always dressed in black, like a widow and had a crocheted black shawl which she always wore fastened with an antique brooch. She wore a mop cap with streamers of ribbon which tied under the chin and she never took the hat off, not even in the house. All she ever seemed to do was stand in that window at the back of the house and stare out into the garden at the birds, which she loved to watch.' Sheila, by now astounded, had a witness to this strange but true story as a friend of hers was in the shop at the time. This same friend had heard the story of the old widow in black and between them they simply could not believe their ears. Sheila never did tell the visitor to the shop that day that she had seen her father's old aunt, as the lady was obviously not for turning, as they say. Sheila herself marvelled at it and pondered whether this was some sort of time slip or recording of past events, as this lady did not die in the cottage but passed away in another town where she came from. She did also wonder, though, if this spirit was merely one in visitation, returning to somewhere she had spent many a happy time.

The apparitions and poltergeist phenomena continued through the years and they are too numerous to mention in this short extract from Sheila's diary of events. Ranging from full-blown apparitions (the Victorian lady in black lacy bonnet and shawl, monk-like figures, soldiers in the garden) to ethereal, misty, shapeless forms, and a host of poltergeist acts, including cobblestone throwing, pots and pans smashing, furniture moving, mirrors breaking and light bulbs shattering, not to mention strange smells, phantom voices and icy breezes, this cottage clearly holds many mysteries. Sheila has tried to find out who the previous owners might have been and to investigate their stories, hoping to find a clue as to who these people are, or were. At one point, whilst investigating under the staircase (where she later discovered the indoor well and what looks like a part of a small cellar area) she found what she thought were human bone fragments and the remains of an old shoe. She jokes in her diary at the time that 'maybe someone had been done in and hidden in the cellar!'

In 1981 Sheila became quite ill, life threateningly so, but one of the last-recorded sightings in her book was that of a man in seventeenth-century garb – breeches, waistcoat, frilly shirt, long cuffs, buckled shoes and ringletted wig. This well-dressed visitor was seen just twice in a certain armchair in her front room, her dog Ben also seeing this same 'something' and howling atrociously, she tells us.

Many years have passed since Sheila first wrote her book on Windmill Cottage and as we sat talking to her of those experiences we were bound to ask if she still saw these 'others' in her home to this day. She looked at us for a long time before she answered and then told us that she has a deep faith and belief in the spirit world, and that the older she got the more she saw. Occasionally, she feels frightened at some of the nightly visitors gathered around her bed, and at other times she is resolute that these are merely lost souls who may need help and comfort as they search in vain for their loved ones, who they feel may still be here and instead find only strangers in their home. How beautifully poignant, and perhaps true.

We must admit that as she showed us from room to room we too felt a growing presence of something nearby, watching, waiting. In one of the rooms upstairs next to a spare bedroom we felt the iciest chill as soon as we opened the door. It was like stepping through something unearthly and with this impenetrable cold came a feeling of intense dread, as if something was about to happen, like the heaviness in the atmosphere that we can sometimes feel before a thunderstorm materialises and lightening strikes.

We are sure that as you read this you will marvel at why on earth anyone would want to continue living in a place so obviously 'alive' with ghosts. But from our own experience we can tell you: because it's fascinating, other worldly, almost spiritually uplifting at times and never, ever dull!

*name and location protected

Mowbreck Hall, Medlar With Wesham

For many centuries Mowbreck Hall, five miles south of Kirkham, was the home of the powerful Westby family, a daughter of which married into the neighbouring Haydock family of Cottam. But it was not to be a long and happy marriage for she died young, leaving widower Vivian Haydock as the master of Mowbreck Hall.

Sadly long gone, razed to the ground by a great fire, the once magnificent twelfth-century hall was long reputed to be the haunt of several spectres, not least a grisly, blood-soaked head that terrified all who saw it.

In the sixteenth century, religious intolerance flourished throughout the land, and the Catholic suppression was at its height. It was on the dark night of All Hallows Eve 1583 that father Haydock made his way to the secret chapel to perform mass. Bedecked in his ritual vestments he lent at prayer before the alter, but as he looked up toward the candlelit crucifix it was not a vision of godliness he saw, but the ghastly site of a gory phantom head which he recognised as that of his son, George Haydock. As he watched, paralysed by fear, the gruesome spectre uttered the words 'Tristita Vestra Vertetur in Gaudium' – the Haydock motto, meaning 'your sorrow shall be turned into joy'. Father Haydock collapsed with shock, the terror of the vision being too much for him to comprehend, and he died shortly afterwards. His body rests beneath the chapel at Cottam Hall.

Unbeknownst to him, his son George had been arrested in London under the laws of the land, a lapsed Catholic named Hankinson having given him up to the authorities, and he had been incarcerated in the Tower to await trial. Fifteen months later he was condemned for high treason after re-affirming his faith and declaring the Queen a heretic; he was hung, drawn and quartered in February 1584. After death his head was allegedly brought back to the North West and taken to Cottam Hall, where it remained in the chapel as a relic of martyrdom, before being removed and taken to Lane End House, Mawdesley, the home of Thomas Hinch, where it remains today. Although it has been suggested that the skull does not belong to George Haydock but instead to a Cistercian monk from Whalley who was hanged in 1537, the related tale is the generally accepted version.

The appearance of the ghoulish head, floating in mid air above the old alter, is said to have been witnessed on many occasions since, most notably around Halloween, the time of the first manifestation, its glowing hue filling the area with an otherworldly glow and the vision of blood seeping from its dried lips.

Contemporary records of ghostly encounters date back to 1955 when John Waterhouse told the *Blackpool Gazette* how he had endured disembodied footsteps in the hall, believed to have been those of a former butler who had committed suicide by hanging. In the 1960s the house was renovated and opened to the public as a country club. The owners, Mr and Mrs Ellis Kit, reported hearing a variety of strange sounds at night which they could not explain, including the footfalls of the phantom butler. The disturbances reached their peak when poltergeist activity broke out, causing items to move around of their own accord, with the result that staff members became increasingly scared. Father Bamber of Dodding Green, Kendal, was called in to quiet the spirits and under his guidance an old concealed priest hide was re-opened in an attempt to lay the ghosts. All seemed peaceful until the following New Year's Eve when angry footsteps were heard ascending the staircase and entering the old priest hide!

Basil Newby, Blackpool entertainment entrepreneur, lived at the hall during the height of the hauntings, and it was his home for seven years. When the *Blackpool Gazette* interviewed him about the ghosts of Mowbreck Hall in early 2008 he recalled that the housekeeper, Evelyn, would avoid the chapel at all costs, after seeing the horrific head. A painting of Lord Derby, one-time owner of the Hall, also seemed to have a haunting presence as it 'watched' with moving eyes. Basil told us that 'Lord Derby had a hunting lodge and a graveyard for his dogs under and oak tree. There were stories that his ghost would walk around the grounds with the dogs following. One night we were camping out and my friend saw a figure pass the lawn with dogs, but he did not know the story of Lord Derby'. Ken and Faye Newby bought the hall in the 1960s, they often heard whistling in rooms which were vacant and locked. Upon opening them the noise would move into the next room, and then the next.

After the building closed to the public it became derelict; a draughty and inhospitable haunting ground for the gruesome head, the phantom butler and Lord Derby. Perhaps shades of the past still lingered there after the living had deserted the place, and whether the fire of recent years, bringing an end to the hall itself, has brought their activity to a final close, or whether they still roam the site of the once grand country house?

Lytham Hall, Lytham

Standing in grounds of approximately 80 acres, Lytham Hall is a Grade 1 listed Georgian house built in the Palladian style. Prior to its construction, a Jacobean manor house was built on the site by Sir Cuthbert Clifton who purchased the manor of Lytham in 1605. Even further back, in the 12th century, an old Benedictine priory once stood on these ancient grounds. The building you see today was built by John Carr of York for Thomas Clifton between 1752 and 1764 and is now considered by some to be 'the finest Georgian house in the county.'

The Hall is now maintained jointly by the Lytham Town Trust and the Heritage Trust for the North West (HTNW). The Friends of Lytham Hall are also actively involved in the welfare of the hall and it is their desire to return this hall to its original splendour.

There are many superb details of elegant Georgian architecture contained within this old hall, but it is in the long gallery, which is part of the original old Jacobean hall, that the 'White Lady of Lytham Hall' is reputed to be seen. As far back as the Second World War, nurses and convalescing servicemen who were housed there reported seeing a 'white lady' as she wafted along the gallery, only to disappear at the far end of it. Since then scores of visitors have reported seeing her and are convinced that she is not of this world.

Kathleen Eyre, in her 1989 book *Lancashire Ghosts*, informs us that she was a frequent visitor to the hall when the last remaining member of the Clifton family, Mrs Violet Clifton, resided there briefly from the late 1950s to the early 1960s. Whilst she admits to not actually seeing a single thing herself, she does admit fleeing the long gallery on many occasions 'with scalp prickling and goose pimples rising like Alps.'

As well as the white lady, two other unidentified spirits have been seen on the top floor of the south wing where the bedrooms are housed. One such room, a dressing room decorated with panelling from the previous Jacobean house, is said to be haunted by the ghost of Sir Cuthbert (perhaps he disapproves of his panelling being moved?) – and another room – the Duke of Norfolk's room which is described as being small and dark – is said to house the ghost of someone with heavy footsteps. This same room, it is alleged, has a door which opens by itself and often the ominous sound of dragging chains can be heard in the same area just outside the door.

It seems that during the 1930s this once magnificent stately home came to be known as a 'sad house', as during that time it was boarded up and left almost derelict by the last remaining relatives of the Clifton family. Although the current building is now undergoing major restoration and refurbishment, sadly this historic old hall of Lytham rarely sees as many visitors, save for its Sunday openings for tours of the house and the occasional event or wedding celebration. It does seem though that sightings are becoming rarer, perhaps because of the lack of actual visitors to the hall, and one could further speculate that the ghost or ghosts of Lytham Hall may soon be left to roam alone and unseen.

MAINS HALL, LITTLE SINGLETON

Tucked away in the historic village of Singleton, only 5 miles from bustling Blackpool's town centre, lies the Grade II listed manor known as Mains Hall. Thought to be originally a medieval long house, the current façade, now quite unremarkable in its style, bears no resemblance to its original construction of timber frame and wattle and daub. Hidden beneath the layers of subsequent centuries of 'restoration', the real heart of the old hall still lies hidden, waiting to give up its secrets to those who know where to look.

The hall has been inhabited by many famous families, the best known of which are the Heskeths of Maynes, who were related to the

Heskeths of Rufford Old Hall near Ormskirk in Lancashire. William Hesketh purchased the hall from Lady Alice, Countess of Derby in 1602, but it is believed that he and possibly earlier generations of Heskeths had been tenants here for many years previously. The Heskeths lived here for over 350 years, a magnificent reign by any standard. Famous visitors include Cardinal Allen, whose sister Elizabeth was married to William Hesketh, then tenant of the hall. It is written that Cardinal Allen hid here during his clandestine visits from Douai in France, and indeed several priest hides can still be found within the old hall. Another famous family emerged after a dearth of males in the Hesketh family forced James Hesketh to take the name of Fitzherbert Brockholes, the most famous of which, Maria Fitzherbert, it is believed found comfort and shelter here during her later years as the 'ex bride' of George IV. Historians confirm that the Prince himself visited Maria here away from the speculation and gossip of the courts and of London society.

This short historical backdrop provides some insight perhaps as to who these other worldly visitors may be who haunt Mains Hall. For many years locals have talked of the old hall and knew of its notoriety in haunting terms. However, it is in this decade that the most prolific ghost stories have been reported, particularly as the hall was once a fine country house hotel, with literally hundreds of visitors, each with their own stories to tell.

Mains Hall appears on old maps as 'Monks Hall', and with good reason. It is believed that a group of lay brothers with links to nearby Cockersand Abbey were tenant farmers here for many years. Although no records have been found yet as to who actually built the hall, it is speculated that monks were the first known inhabitants of some sort of dwelling here. Visitors to the old hotel reported seeing their shadowy, cowled figures in the gardens and they are also reported inside the house too. An ancient and blackened oak door has been rescued from what used to be the Hesketh family's chapel and if you dare to touch this door it is said to vibrate beneath your trembling fingers. It is carved over the top with a now very famous motif – that of the Knight's Templar cross – perhaps pre-dating the Hesketh's reign into the time that the Monks lived here. A nun is often seen fleetingly passing by in one of the upper chambers – again, the Hesketh family had more than one 'sister' take her vows. In fact, one famous Hesketh lady of Mains Hall was the Abbess of the Benedictine Dames of Ghent. She was buried in 1809 in the Catholic chapel of Fernyhalgh, where a beautiful marble tablet inscribed to her memory still stands today. One could speculate that she returns in visitation only, to her birthplace and real home.

Roger Griffiths, now living in Tenerife but originally from London, stayed here in the autumn of 1990 as a guest in the then hotel. He had come to visit friends who lived locally and they all went out for dinner on the night he stayed at Mains Hall. He returned late and had a drink at the bar, then went up to his bedroom, Room 3, a lovely double room that overlooked the main drive and gardens. There was no mention of ghosts or other such spookiness prior to his ascent to his room, and as he was not local he had no knowledge of the hall other than that it was an old manor house. He slept well, but was awoken in the early hours by the feeling that there was someone in the room. He describes an icy chill in the air and he tugged hard at the duvet and blankets on his bed, pulling them closer to his chin for warmth. The duvet would not budge, so he sat up slightly and tugged harder. He peered into the darkness without turning on the bedside light and was shocked to see something or someone small, like a female child, at the foot of his bed. He quickly retracted his feet (he is a tall man almost 6 feet 4 inches) and sat bolt upright with his knees under his chin, staring at the shape at the foot of his bed. Within seconds it vanished, and although petrified he continued to sit upright for at least half an hour, he tells us, in simple disbelief. The next morning he solemnly declared to his friends that he had been woken by 'something' sitting on his bed, 'something' that looked like a small girl, to which they all roared with laughter, being locals, and informed him: ' Oh you've seen one of the ghosts then!'

In another part of the hall where the old bar used to be housed, a cheerful Cavalier type was once seen by as many as twelve hotel guests at one time – a rare occurrence by any standards. The group of twelve were all staying together as one group when someone asked who the 'other odd looking gentleman was, and was he with us?' At that time, all twelve people agreed that they could see the same man in what looked like to them to be fancy dress. Other guests have reported seeing what look like soldiers in old fashioned uniforms with swords. Local legend tells us that during the Jacobite Rebellion marauding troops broke in here and insisted on being 'entertained' by the lady of the house. A swordfight was alleged to have taken place and one unfortunate lost his life on the grand staircase. Could this be the same 'soldier'? It is known that a Thomas Hesketh, 'a captain of horse under Charles II', was slain at the skirmish at Brindle, near Preston, in 1651' could it be his troubled spirit that returns to defend his home? Shapes are often seen on the Jacobean staircase and there is a deep sense of foreboding in this area – one local workman, Stephen, who came here in 1991 to do some maintenance work, left rather hurriedly, reporting sheer terror and the feeling that he was being jostled whilst working there.

One of the more 'saucy' hauntings, reported by at least two female guests when Mains Hall was a hotel, is the man who gets into bed alongside (so far) only female guests in Room 9 – a downstairs room in the Victorian part of the Hall. This cheeky chappie bestows favours (shall we say politely) upon ladies in this room and in fact one lady who we shall call 'Sarah', not her real name for reasons which seem obvious, booked an extra night here on the strength of the happenings in this room! Actually known as an incubus haunting, this type of thing is not as rare as one would imagine, although while Room 9's gentleman seems relatively harmless, it seems some incubus hauntings can take on a more sinister and sometimes aggressive form.

In an adjoining field a strange-looking building stands alone, deserted and half in ruin. This ancient dovecote has itself been subject to its own haunting. A local gentleman, David Summerville, who has lived in this area for many years, and knew Mains Hall well in his youth, couldn't wait to tell us of his experience as a young lad, playing in and around the old hall. In the early 1950s, he and a friend, who holidayed in this area with their families, used to trespass into the field where the dovecote lay. Their games were usually of the same vein – climbing inside the dovecote using the pigeon holes built into the brickwork for footholds, in an attempt to reach the top. As they played here happily on many occasions, they considered themselves lucky that the owners of the hall had not come into the field and spied them. However, one day, whilst inside the ancient brick pigeon house, they looked down from their advantageous climbing position to see a man, described as wearing old-fashioned trousers (britches) cut off at the knee, boots, flat cap and waistcoat and, more alarmingly, sporting a shotgun half cocked over his arm. Fearing themselves to be in terrible trouble, they remained inside, clinging to the sides for dear life, as the man stood silently in the main body of the rounded building, not looking left or right or indeed upwards. After a minute or two, the man silently left and the boys very quickly, now with most tired fingers from clinging on for so long, jumped down and peeped out of the dovecote to see in which direction the man was travelling in order that they would run in the opposite direction to avoid 'capture'. To their amazement, in a field of approximately four acres with nothing save the dovecote in its centre, they saw nothing; the man had completely vanished. The boys reasoned later when they returned home to their holiday home nearby (rather swiftly, our storyteller remarked), that it would not have been possible for any living man to have travelled the full length of the field so quickly and be out of sight within minutes! Suitably spooked, they now believe they had seen a ghost, and indeed others have reported a gamekeeper type who is often seen in this area of what would have once been the estate of Mains Hall – extensive in its day. Not only has this man been seen out perhaps continuing his duties as gamekeeper, albeit on another astral plane, he often appears in the old kitchen of the hall, where we are told the game room and butler's pantry were once housed.

One of the more interesting and truly unique stories around one of the ghosts of Mains Hall came to light only recently and involves Adele personally. Here she takes up the story: My husband and I first moved into what used to be Room 4 (now named the Tudor Room) which overlooks the beautiful River Wyre. Guests when staying in this room often complained the next morning of having been 'disturbed' throughout the night – some reported a child sitting on the bed, others spoke of a male presence which seemed to unnerve them. Some mentioned a dark lady and I saw this lady myself on many occasions. She always looked the same: she was clad in a dress, dark in colour with a white collar and beads around the neckline. Her hair was sleeked back, dark, and she had pale skin and red lips. The dress looked like a three-quarter length evening dress one would wear even today. She always looked so sad and melancholic.

As another bedroom was finished following refurbishment we moved out of this room into another, just up the stairs from the old Room 4. I thought that I had seen the last of 'my lady' as I had now moved out! However, one morning as I descended the stairs I saw, in the corridor to my left, just outside the old Room 4, a figure in black. I paced downstairs and up towards that end of the corridor and I called out 'Hello … who's that?' No reply. I hesitated outside Room 4, then with some trepidation opened the door and there she was – 'my lady' looking out towards the river! I slammed the door and ran downstairs, shouting for my husband as I went.

As the days went by I began to feel a strong affiliation with her, even coming up with a name which continually popped into my head each time I saw her: Lily. My morning greeting became, 'Morning Lily, how are you today?' I even lit a candle and put a vase of lilies at the top of the staircase in her honour. My story would have remained merely an interesting anecdote to tell friends until a fateful event occurred. I had been researching the history of the hall and in so doing had put a piece on a website on the internet inviting past residents or anyone else who knew about the history of the manor house to contact me. Eventually a lady who had lived here in the 1940s called Frances Green contacted me and we had several conversations, first online then over the telephone. She was highly amused to hear that we had so many ghostly 'others' residing here with us and as I began to describe in detail how 'my lady' appeared to me, she became very animated. 'The lady you describe so vividly sounds to me like the wife of a gentleman who used to lived there – she only ever wore black, she was very fashion conscious and wore her hair in the style of the day, sleeked back and tied in a knot at the back of her head. She took great care of her appearance, wearing the pale make up of the day and bright red lipstick. She often wore a dress with a lacy collar, but she also favoured a double string of pearls too. She often spent her nights looking out of the window awaiting her husband's return from business.'

'Was her name Lily, by any chance?' I queried. The phone fell silent for some time. 'Hello … . are you still there?' I said. 'I can't believe what you are telling me', she gasped. 'It was my mother who was called Lily and she was not only the head housekeeper here, she was also a great friend and source of comfort to this lady of the house in times when she was lonely or distraught.' These two women formed a strong bond and Frances recollects that the lady of the house would often call out to her domestic helper when she wished to talk. 'Lily', she would call out towards the part of the house where Lily resided, 'Lily, are you there?'

What a strange quirk of fate; I had found out who 'my lady' was and the name I had 'heard' or associated with her – Lily – who was in fact a dear friend and confidante in times when she needed a shoulder to cry on. Some months later the local *Gazette* newspaper ran Frances's story and I was please to see how affectionately she remembered her own times at Mains Hall as well as those of her own mother. Neither Frances nor I can truly explain what happened here, nor can we say why Lily still comes to 'visit', though Frances was convinced that her mother would return here to Mains Hall, a place she always loved. I still see her form in the same places on frequent occasions and still I greet her with the usual 'Good Morning Lily', though I think we both know that is not her name.

Whatever else, the haunting of Mains Hall is not a new phenomenon. Old newspaper cuttings dating back as far as the late 1940s and 50s. tell stories of mysterious unearthly visitors to the Hall. In June 1950, the then owner, Mr Arthur Hall, a local business man and cinema owner told the local newspaper of how he and his wife were frequently wakened by noises in the night and were left 'waiting … feeling sure that someone was near'.

But the legend of the ghosts of Mains Hall goes back even further. According to an old book by Allen Clarke written in 1917 entitled *The Windmill Land* the hall was shunned by locals, as it was derelict and considered haunted even then. Mains Hall may no longer be derelict, as major restoration continues and the historic hall continues to give up its secrets even now, but haunted … ah yes, and most likely to remain so forever.

Robins Lane, Carleton

Approximately four miles outside of Blackpool town centre in a suburb known as Carleton, lies Robins Lane. On maps it is shown as a small lane running north from Blackpool Road in the Carleton area, but in reality there is another Robins Lane which is slightly disjointed and runs northwards towards the Bispham area. Both lanes lead into new housing estates but once upon a time there were only fields, farms and ponds. If you trace historical maps you will find that this now fractured lane was a continuous track that linked man farms in the vicinity. It is believed that this old track was possibly used in conjunction with the agricultural market which was held here in Carleton many decades ago.

In the late 1960s, a young boy named James Young and his friend Michael, then both aged about 12, were riding their bikes in the lanes one early winter's evening. Dusk was falling and the boys, who had been in this area many times playing around the fields and ponds, sometimes fishing there, made their way home towards the Bispham Road end of Robins Lane. As they rode their bikes furiously down the dirt track they both looked up in amazement as they saw a tall, dark man in what they described as a 'cloak-like coat pulled up high at the neck ... quite old fashioned looking.' They both pulled up quickly and stopped. As they both said later, 'The man was wearing such odd clothes, of course we stopped to stare!' As they watched the man (whose face they could not see clearly as he had his back to them) he slowly drifted into the hedge and out onto the other side, his bodily form going straight through the branches. Unable to move for a few seconds due to sheer terror, both the boys looked at each other and then silently back towards the dark shape, which now seemed to be drifting along the other side of the hedgerow. As suddenly as the mysterious stranger had appeared he literally disappeared in front of them, and this time, whilst again looking at one another and saying excitedly 'Did you see that!!', they shot off as fast as their little legs would take them in the opposite direction – a much longer way home towards Cleveleys where they lived. James and Michael were certainly spooked, but not scared enough to stay away. In fact James states that

they still frequented this area for some years after and during that time saw the apparition once more. The second time they saw it, dressed in the same attire, the shadowy form seemed to rise up alongside them on the other side of the hedge as they rode their bicycles northbound towards the Bispham area. This time they both jumped off their bikes, and traversed the ditch in an effort to run alongside the figure, hoping to gain a better look at the man's face. Once again, the dark stranger drifted through the hedgerows and silently swept ahead of them, before disappearing some feet ahead. Still shaken, they both swore that they would never tell anyone what they had seen unless, as James put it, 'Something terrible happened to anyone walking in the lane', at which point they were prepared to come forward and tell all. James, now 54 years of age, says he has never seen another ghost before or since, but he is absolutely convinced that what he saw was not a 'real' person in the living sense.

In this particular area of the lane there have been many sightings of this ghostly form dressed in the same dark 'cloak-like' clothing, but there have also been reports of other equally disconcerting ghostly shapes, all of which cause local people to shun this entire area, especially after dark. Many are aware of the legends surrounding these ghostly apparitions and as the interest in all things paranormal seems to continue, more and more people are coming forward to report their sightings, whereas once they felt they should keep silent about such things. Some of these supernatural encounters could even originate from more ancient times, as many people, including local author Graham Evans in his 1989 book *Places, Legends and Tales of The Fylde*, refer to something called 'the boggart of Robins Lane', suggesting this particular spirit may have been around for some time. A 'boggart' is a medieval term for a 'devil, green goblin or mischievous ghost'. It can also be an agricultural sprite, sometimes known as a 'brownie', often responsible for playing pranks on farms or stealing implements from agricultural fields. Given that this local area was once very much an agricultural space and markets were held in the vicinity, it is interesting to note the type of activity that has been reported here, and moreover, what this ghost looks like in just one of its terrifying incarnations.

Our 'boggart' received the most publicity in 1936, after it was first described as 'The Green Ghost of Carleton'. The local paper, the *Blackpool Evening Gazette*, reported the story of a taxi driver, one Harry Hodges, who whilst dropping off his fare near the newly constructed Carleton Crematorium gates, saw the horrific green, glowing face of an old man, 'with sunken eyes, long dark hair, a Punch-like nose and prominent chin'. His female passenger also saw the phantom and let out a shriek fit to wake the nearby dead in the graveyard. This so-called green ghost vanished in front of the taxi and Harry at first made no attempt to set off into the shadows to look for the form. Likewise, the lady passenger who had hailed the taxi in the North Shore area of Blackpool asking to be taken to Robins Lane, made a swift exit herself ... without paying the cabbie I hasten to add! Although Harry did eventually pluck up the courage to go and look for his lady passenger, she was not around long enough to verify his terrifying encounter. A frightening tale by all accounts, but the story of the ghost of Robins Lane does not end here. Many have seen other things, including an ominous red hand rising up out of a pond (red hands were once carved over door lintels on some farms, according to local historians, and although their exact meaning is unclear it is generally considered a warning sign of some description); a white mist which brushes past people whilst travelling along the road nearest to the Carleton area of the lane; and an ethereal green mist which some have captured on camera. It is recorded that an old woman was battered to death here several years prior to Harry Hodges' first encounter in 1936; however, the description he gave at the time bears no resemblance to that of a little old lady.

So what of the hideous green-faced ghost, the cloaked man who has been seen, not to mention the swirling green mists, the red hand and shadowy forms? Could it be that the Green Ghost of Carleton has more than one incarnation? Is this the original 'boggart' which Fylde legend speaks of? This true ghost story perhaps deserves further investigation ... if you dare!

SINGLETON HALL, SINGLETON

Now a luxury development of contemporary apartments which offer the discerning country gent modern comforts in a traditional setting, Singleton Hall has survived where countless other mansions of its type fall into ruin. It is inevitable that old country houses of grandeur must succumb to the ravages of modern tastes, and either adapt or cease to be Singleton Hall it seems is one of the lucky ones! But has the unerring onslaught of development wiped away the shades of an ancient past, or have the ghosts of days long gone survived the cataclysmic alterations ...

The extravagant gothic mansion, with its gargoyles and fine stonework, was constructed in 1855 for the family of Thomas Miller, a wealthy cotton magnate and collector of art. He had become a chief partner in his father's successful spinning empire, Horrocks, Miller and Company, in Preston in 1846 and his new-found fortune allowed him the indulgence of a lavish country home.

The mills owned by the company employed many hundreds of workers, and Miller was an amiable boss, famed for introducing education for workers children and pensions for staff. With an acute eye for architectural excellence, Thomas did not stop after construction of the grand house was complete; he also commissioned many of Singleton's other noted buildings, including the Miller Arms public house and St Anne's Church – both distinctively styled in the same vein. Upon his death in 1865 his son succeeded ownership of Singleton Hall.

We were intrigued by the development taking place at the hall in 2006 when we came across an old stone fireplace in a reclamation yard which, it was said, had come from Singleton Hall. At the time one of us was about to undertake a country restoration project and was very tempted to purchase the fireplace, but was concerned about what may be lingering in the rubble. We are always dubious about old architecture; it seems to 'hold on' to the vibrations of times past, and we are always careful to note what may have occurred in their vicinity before introducing them to our own homes.

Only days later we were talking to a colleague, who wishes to remain anonymous, about the fireplace and she told us that she had been to view the new apartments at the hall a few days before. Having a keen interest in ghostly tales, she enquired of one of the workmen if any 'odd' happenings had been reported, as building work often 'upsets' spirits which may otherwise lie dormant. She was told that several things had happened which had 'spooked' the stalwart builders, including machinery playing up and things moving around – perhaps Thomas Miller is making sure that everything in the new development is exactly as he wants it!

CHAPTER SIX

SEASIDE SPOOKS

WINDSOR AVENUE, THORNTON

An unassuming house on Windsor Avenue in Thornton was the site of one of the North West's most frightening poltergeist cases back in the early 1970s, when the Ross family were tormented and terrified by an unseen assailant whose reign of terror eventually drove them from their own home, and continued until 1996.

The story became widely known thanks to coverage in the *Blackpool Gazette*, which christened it 'The Thornton Thing'. The incumbent Ross family described how the 'thing' would attack them while in bed, grabbing at the covers and disturbing them as they tried to sleep. The sinister phantasm would breathe menacingly in their ears, and announce its presence with a spectral scent like an open grave.

As the happenings increased, that family fled, leaving their home behind. It was years later in 1988 that Frank Jones and his family moved into the house. Although he had been warned about the legendary ghost Frank did not believe in such things and ignored the tales of 'The Thing'. But he should perhaps have heeded the words of those who warned him away, for its was only a short time before he too found himself at the mercy of the phantom predator.

He described his experiences to the *Blackpool Gazette* in early 2008, telling them: 'there was a lot of banging and an earthy smell in the house, one night I was lying in bed and a mist came across the room. I wanted to shout out at it but I couldn't get the words out. My face seemed to be paralysed'.

Other members of the family soon shared his experiences; Frank's daughter Maureen told the *Gazette* that she had witnessed footsteps on the staircase, taps turning on by themselves and cupboard doors banging violently. After many sleepless nights and with the ghostly presence making itself felt on a variety of occasions, Frank eventually decided to call in some help and he turned to the Spiritualist Church.

A medium from Fleetwood's branch of the Spiritualists went into the building to conduct a spirit cleansing. She described the ghost of a man who was trapped between two worlds and unable to move on. Following her ceremony the visitations stopped and the activities of 'The Thing' ceased.

In many cases of poltergeist attack, the focus seems to be on a particular person, often a young child or teenager, but in this case the entity seems to have attached itself to the building rather than the family, allowing it to flourish in the company of both the Ross family, and later the Jones.

KILGRIMOL, LYTHAM ST ANNES

In his book *Ghosts, Traditions and Legends of Old Lancashire*, author Ken Howarth describes a church which reputedly stood on a precarious stretch of land not far south of Blackpool town once known as 'Kilgrimol'. The village of Kilgrimol was allegedly founded by Viking settlers around the year 900.

According to the tale, the building and its associated cemetery (presumably inhabited?) were swept away into the sea during a torrential storm, and it is said that when the same troubled weather conditions are replicated today, the distant sound of ghostly bells may be heard ringing from beneath the raging waves. It seems that the phantom villagers are still going about their business, albeit beneath the raging waves of the turbulent sea ...

An alternative version of this well-known local folk tale states that the church at Kilgrimol was swallowed up in a violent earthquake, although this seems unlikely, earthquakes of that ferocity being pretty uncommon in Lytham. A more likely version holds that the church

was actually a 'Keeill' – an ancient Pagan/Celtic Christian church
built from an upturned boat, possibly on the site of an ancestral burial
place. It is far easier to imagine this kind of less substantial erection
subsiding into the sea than something constructed of stone.

It is true that the name of the famed area can be found in
contemporary local useage such as in the street name 'Kilgrimol
Gardens' and the school 'Kilgrimol School for Boys', so perhaps
the old tale of the ghostly peel of the phantom bells deserves some
credence?

The tramway, Blackpool & Fleetwood

Three phantoms are said to frequent the famous promenade and tramway. While during the hours of daylight thousands of tourists flock to
buy sticks of candy rock and ride the donkeys, in the twilight hours

when the neon façade is out, and the moon casts long shadows on the tramways, the sound of a long-gone tram carriage can still be heard, trundling along the tracks, as it did so many years ago.

Many local residents have investigated the ghostly sound, which they have witnessed most frequently between the hours of 2 a.m. and sunrise, but have been unable to account for it. Early one morning an inspector heard the unmistakable sound of an approaching carriage and turned to see it, lights ablaze in the fog, trundle toward him. After signalling for the tram to stop so that he could board, it dematerialised in front of him.

A local Blackpool resident named as Mrs R. Dugdale is quoted in *North Country Ghosts & legends*, as saying 'we heard a tram coming, but there was nothing to be seen. The noise increased as the tram got closer and, as it passed, we all got our feet wet from the rainwater thrown up from between the rails, yet no visible tram passed us!'. This incident is recorded as having occurred on the stretch of tramway opposite the Claremont Hotel, minutes from North Pier. Mrs Dugdale also commented that she had often heard the 'ghost tram's air-horn sounding in the early hours of the morning as it left Manchester Square; yet on each occasion when she had looked, there had been no tram to account for the sound.

Another tale tells of a phantom tram worker whose restless spirit glides along the promenade after coming out of a private gateway. Carrying a lighted storm lantern, the spectre is only seen on stormy nights when the waves are pounding on the seafront and all but the bravest of souls are tucked up in bed, still lighting the way for those unfortunates who may be lost in the sea mists. According to author Terence Whitaker, he is said to be a former points man who joined the Blackpool Tram Company at the age of 14, and worked, almost continually, on the lines all his life.

Further up the tramway system, at Fleetwood, the ghost of an old man has been seen sitting beside the track lines near the lighthouse. When approached the melancholy spirit wanders across the road and pauses to peer out to sea, before vanishing and returning to the land of the dead once again, who he is and why his spirit haunts here, are a mystery.

JUMPER, LYTHAM ST ANNES

Whilst carrying out research for this book we were contacted by many people from various parts of Blackpool and its surrounding areas with stories of unusual hauntings. This story, concerning a shop on Clifton Street in the bustling seaside town of Lytham St Annes, comes from Debi Clark.

Our correspondent states that she has lived in Lancashire for the last 12 years and has always had a strange uncanny feeling of being watched by unseen eyes whilst browsing in the shop, particularly in the area of the changing rooms. She recently commented upon this to the manageress, who informed her that they do have strange things happening in the building, including stock being moved from the shelves overnight and being piled up in front of the door, making access difficult in the morning. Other phenomena include display material being tampered with and shadowy figures sighted on the second floor where the toilets are located.

The activity is blamed on the presence of the unquiet spirits of a mother and son who were connected to the building in life. Apparently the haunting disturbances became so bad in the past that an exorcism was performed which seemed to dispel the phenomena for some years, but recently the spirits have become restless again, often causing an anomalous smell of smoke when they are present. Could this smell be a clue as to the reason for the haunting at the shop? It has been impossible to obtain further details on this particular case and at the time of writing it remains unsolved.

BIBLIOGRAPHY

Publications:
Ghosts of North West England by Peter Underwood, Fontana, 1978.
The Ghosts of Lancashire by Muriel Armand, Print Origination, 1993
Supernatural Lancashire by Peter Hough, Hale, 2003.
Ghosts of the North by Melanie Warren & Tony Wells, Broadcast Books, 1995.
Lancashire's Ghosts & Legends by Terence Whitaker, Granada, 1982.
Ghosts, Traditions & Legends of Old Lancashire by Ken Howarth, Sigma Leisure, 1993.
The Haunted Pub Guide by Guy Lyon Playfair, Harrap, 1985.
North Country Ghosts & Legends by Terence Whitaker, Grafton Books, 1988.
Lancashire Ghosts by Kathleen Eyre, Dalesman, 1989.
Haunted Halls of Lancashire by Keith Hassall & Mike Firth, Lancashire Books, 1990.
Around Haunted Manchester by Peter Portland, AMCD Publishers, 2002.
Jason Karl's Great Ghost Hunt by Jason Karl, New Holland Publishers, 2004.
21st Century Ghosts by Jason Karl, New Holland Publishers, 2007.
Haunted Places of Lancashire by Jason Karl, Countryside Books, 2006.
An Illustrated History of the Haunted World by Jason Karl, New Holland Publishers, 2007.
The Secret World of Witchcraft by Jason Karl, New Holland Publishers, 2008.
Preston's Haunted Heritage by Jason Karl & Adele Yeomans, Palatine Books, 2007.
An Account of Mains Hall in the time of Queen Elizabeth I (taken from papers: The Historic Society of Lancashire and Cheshire, Vol. 5 1852-Thornber Rev. W, published by Historic Society of Lancashire and Cheshire), 1853.

The Windmill Land by Allen Clarke, J M Dent, 1917.

Places, Legends and Tales of The Fylde by Graham Evans, Creek Publishers, 1989.

Lancashire's Architectural Heritage by John Champness, Lancashire County Planning Dept, 1988.

The Parish of Bispham, A History of the County of Lancaster: Volume 7 by William Farrer & J. Brownbill (editors), Victoria County History, 1912.

The History of the Parish of Bispham in the County of Lancaster by Henry Fishwick, Chetham Society, 1887.

The Fylde in the 1930s and '40s by Catherine Rothwell, Hendon Publishing Co Ltd. 1984.

Albert Clayton's Garstang and Fylde Album by Albert Clayton, Silver Fox Publishing, 1990.

Periodicals:

Blackpool Gazette, various dates

Websites

www.atmosfearuk.com

www.jasondexterkarl.com

www.mainshall.co.uk

www.supernaturalevents.co.uk

www.laffinthedark.com

www.louistussaudswaxworks.co.uk

www.blackpoolpleasurebeach.com

www.theeagleandchild.co.uk

www.blackpool.gov.uk/grundyartgallery

www.blackpoolgrand.co.uk

www.wintergardensblackpool.co.uk

www.theoldcoachhouse.co.uk

www.ghostresearch.org

www.tyldesley.co.uk

www.poulton-le-fylde-hcs.co.uk

www.lythamhall.org

www.british-history.ac.uk

www.blackpoolcircusschool.co.uk